Oops

What We Learn
When Our Teaching Fails

Brenda Miller Power

and

Ruth Shagoury Hubbard

Coeditors

Stenhouse Publishers
York, Maine

It's not enough to fail. You have to come to feel your failure, to live it through, to turn it over in your hand, like a stone with strange markings.

James Fenton

Stenhouse Publishers, P.O. Box 360, York, Maine 03909
www.stenhouse.com

A portion of the authors' and editors' earnings are being donated to *Rethinking Schools,* a non-profit newspaper advocating the reform of public schools. Founded ten years ago by classroom teachers and educators, it has a particular focus on issues of equity and social justice.

Library of Congress Cataloging-in-Publication Data

Oops : what we learn when our teaching fails / Brenda Miller Power and Ruth Shagoury Hubbard, coeditors.
    p. cm.
    Includes bibliographical references.
    ISBN 1-57110-027-X (alk. paper)
    1. Teaching—United States—Anecdotes. 2. Failure (Psychology)—Anecdotes. 3. Classroom management—United States—Anecdotes. 4. Teacher-student relationships—United States—Anecdotes. I. Power, Brenda Miller. II. Hubbard, Ruth, 1950– .
    LB1027.058 1996
    371.1'02—dc20   95-46907
                                         CIP

Interior design by Cathy Hawkes
Cover illustration by John O'Brien
Administrative support at University of Maine by Susan Russell
Typeset by Technologies 'N Typography

Manufactured in the United States of America on acid-free paper
03 02 01 00   8 7 6 5 4 3

Contents

Contents

Contents

Introduction

BRENDA MILLER POWER
AND RUTH SHAGOURY HUBBARD

Most teachers are essentially optimists. They have to be to survive. Ours is a profession of dogged individuals who are determined to overcome the long odds against learning in overcrowded, undersupplied classrooms.

But in the midst of such inspiring optimism at every turn, silences simmer. There are many stories we do not tell, because they do not provide hope or inspiration. They are the stories of failure in our teaching, and they are often the stories we carry closest to our hearts. If we tell them at all, it is usually with a happily-ever-after ending: "It was good I lived through that reading group disaster, because it made me change my reading program to the wonderful curriculum I have today."

Perhaps the push toward teaching stories that are always positive is influenced by the "super teachers" immortalized in books and on film in our culture. The idealistic teachers portrayed by actors like Sidney Poitier in *To Sir with Love* or, more recently, Michelle Pfeiffer in *Dangerous Minds* promote the idea that anything is possible in classrooms if teachers just have enough drive, intelligence, and concern for their students. The public has a voracious appetite for these stories. We want to believe that it doesn't take more money to make schools better—it just takes more teachers willing to be heroic.

But for every teacher who makes it to the big screen with her accomplishments, there are dozens more earthbound educators who manage to have their classroom practices published in books and articles. The move toward professional materials written by teachers for teachers is one of the most encouraging changes in education over the past two decades. Teachers are presenting their ideas in their own words to peers, exhorting them to try what has worked for them. These stories from real classrooms help to show teachers what is possible, inspiring others to take similar risks in their teaching, experimenting and sharing what they've learned.

But when we take risks, we are courting failure. What happens when a teacher tries a new method, philosophy, or activity presented in one of these books and it doesn't work well? What happens when the results are disastrous? When a colleague's successful method fails in your classroom, you're left feeling like yesterday's Cheese Whiz. Very few stories of failure and discouragement appear in writing by teachers. These are stories that teachers need to tell—and hear, too. Teachers can find little in the literature that tells them what to do next when an activity stinks up the classroom or what might be learned as they mop up the pieces of a splattered innovation.

In analyzing narratives on whole language/process teaching, Tom Newkirk (1993) wonders if we aren't hurting ourselves with our relentlessly optimistic tone:

> *I wonder if we are not creating the role of "super teacher," one more ideal, without cracks, that creates a sense of inadequacy in all of us. Are there silences in the narratives we tell of our whole language/writing process classrooms? Are we telling everything? Do these consistently upbeat success stories capture the emotional underlife of teaching? I think not.* (p. 23)

In *Oops: What We Learn When Our Teaching Fails*, we want to help transform the image of the "super teacher" by sharing the stories that don't get told, the stories that haunt and sometimes humor us as we continue to try to understand what it means to be a good teacher. Some of these stories are painful, but some will also provoke much laughter as they resonate with the experiences of readers.

Many of the stories in the collection are unfinished in terms of learning from the experience of failure. Authors might not yet know what can be learned from them, and in printing them we hope to show that learning from failure isn't a quick and easy process. Some of these stories do provide learning, but the insights may be ugly and hard to face. They are the stories of racial tension in our classrooms, of hurt feelings among colleagues, of learning activities that work in every classroom but ours.

Our process in compiling the collection was simple. We invited writers and teachers who have served as an inspiration to us when our teaching fails to write about a negative experience in their teaching. We were amazed at how many of these near and distant mentors, many of whom we know only through their published work, were willing to write essays about their teaching mistakes, duds, and disasters. We can only believe the potholes these exemplary teachers encountered in their journeys of learning to teach will be just as helpful as those stories of success we know so well.

In *Composing a Life* (1991), Mary Catherine Bateson seeks to unravel and make sense of the greatest professional failure of her life, her dismissal as dean of faculty at a prestigious private university. In considering her failure, she writes:

When there is a rent in the canvas, a discord in the harmony, a betrayal, it is important not only to recover but to discover a new and inclusive pattern of meaning. Part of the task of composing a life is the artist's need to find a way to take what is simply ugly and, instead of trying to deny it, to use it in the broader design. There is a famous story about a Chinese master painting a landscape. Just as he is nearly finished, a drop of ink falls on the white scroll, and the disciples standing around him gasp, believing the scroll is ruined. Without hesitating, the master takes the finest of hair brushes and, using the tiny globe of ink already fallen, paints a fly hovering in the foreground of the landscape. For a large . . . institution, criticism is like the buzzing of a fly, but the purpose here is to discover grace and meaning in a picture larger still. (p. 113)

This collection is filled with many buzzing flies—forty-seven stories from veteran teachers, and the impact of these stories on their professional lives. These stories reveal humor, pain, wasted energies, and renewed commitment. We hope in presenting them, a larger picture of grace and meaning can be discovered. We most often see ourselves as teachers buzzing against large institutions we may have little control over—bureaucracies, budgets, and resistance to change. But the most challenging threat may reside *in* us, in the silences we hold because we allow only a narrow slice of classroom life to be viewed by peers.

We considered organizing the collection in many different ways—by student age level, theme, magnitude of disaster. . . . In the end, we decided not to force an artificial structure or order on the essays. We want readers to find their own order. You may want to start by reading the pieces by favorite writers you recognize in the table of contents. Or you may want to refer to the indexes in the back of the book, which do list all the essays by grade level or theme. For example, you may choose to peruse all the essays dealing with elementary-level students. Or, if this week your students are breaking out in fist fights during literature discussion groups, you may want to look at all the essays dealing with collaboration and community. This collection may sit on your bedstand for a month as a nightly treat or be read aloud piece by piece in teachers lounges or college classrooms.

Maybe we balk at talking and writing about failure because we've heard too much failure in the air in those teachers' lounges and college classrooms. None of us wants to become one of the many cynics in our profession who believe any new idea or philosophy of teaching that honors and respects learners is ultimately doomed. What we hope this collection does is show the positive possibilities of learning from failure. If we can make sense of failure, we may in the end help create learning communities that are even more respectful of learners and our own needs as teachers. Our goal for this book is that it can expand the conversation of reflection in our profession. By uncovering and writing about the memories we silence, ignore, or bury, we may all find our way down paths previously closed by the boundaries of what we're willing to speak and write about as teachers.

References

Bateson, Mary Catherine. 1991. *Composing a Life.* New York: Atlantic Monthly.

Newkirk, Thomas. 1993. "Silences in Our Teaching Stories." In *Workshop 4: The Teacher as Researcher.* Portsmouth, NH: Heinemann.

Re-Entry Blues

JAMES A. BEANE

In 1990 I had a small book published proposing a new design for the middle school curriculum—thematic units planned from scratch with students, using questions they have about themselves and the world. Not long after, Barbara Brodhagen, a middle school teacher who also happens to be my wife, made arrangements for us to work with a group of eighth-grade students to try out my approach.

As a professor I have spent considerable time in and out of classrooms as a consultant or observer, though my days as a real teacher in a public school are long past. While spending time in classrooms as a visitor involves contact with young people and the structures of schooling, it is a quite different thing to go to the same place every day and live with the consequences of yesterday's actions and today's plans. It did not take long to remember this.

The school year was nearly half completed when we began our project. Knowing each other and their classroom routines well, the students sat at their desks, talking and laughing. I stood up in front of them that first morning, ready to give the first direction for our collaborative planning. As I opened my mouth, I realized in a millisecond of sheer terror that I had no way to get the attention of these students and that since they did not know me, there was no apparent reason they should give it to me. This may seem trivial but there was horror where the What do I do now? of the moment met the professorial But I'm supposed to know how to do this. As it turns out, I did the smartest thing as I turned to the real teacher and said, "Barbara?" Here is my point: she simply stood up and half-said, half-sang, "Good morning." The room was almost instantly quiet.

In that moment I had a sudden revelation. Anyone who leaves classroom teaching for more than three minutes should have a re-entry course before returning. It's not that the skills simply get rusty. It's that they atrophy. And there is a serious loss of "presence," that capacity to *be* in a classroom with confidence that you will be taken seriously. If there had been such a thing as a Constitution for teaching, the re-entry course requirement would certainly have been among the first few amendments.

But this little episode was not even close to the most humbling among the seemingly endless array of re-entry blues I experienced in Barbara's classroom over the next few years. Halfway through the next year, now in a seventh-grade classroom, the group was in the midst of a unit on "the future." Among the questions the students had raised to form the unit were several regarding population growth and the future of their city. I agreed to take on the job of gathering and presenting some information related to these questions.

I planned what was undoubtedly one of the finest lessons in the history of education. First I would show these young people the "J curve" of world population growth, growing so slowly for centuries and then accelerating in the twentieth to make a J. Next I would show the population projections for Madison, not only growing sharply but also involving that peristalsis-like bulge of middle-aged baby boomers moving inexorably toward their elder years. Then we would work in cooperative groups to figure out some of the implications and effects of these shifts on our world and city. Finally, after debriefing the small-group work and just at the end of our time, I would pull all of this together with a breathtaking concept that would stay with these seventh graders for all the days of their lives.

And so it went, through the presentation and the small-group work. As the debriefing proceeded with the students' excellent insights about health care, transportation, taxes, and so on, I kept one eye on the clock, counting down to the perfect timing for my unforgettable concept. Finally, *the* moment! As I ascended into the breathtaking beauty of the big idea, a front-row student who had begun to teeter in her chair sat bolt upright and threw up her lunch on me and two others. Now the bell rang and the class dutifully stood and left the room, leaving behind a messy floor, one sick student, two spattered others, a stunned teacher, and a great concept only half spoken.

Two things stay with me from this. One is that for the life of me I cannot remember what that unforgettable concept was. The other is the terrifying thought that in the middle of that sentence, one student, I hope not speaking for others, had offered up her evaluation of my curriculum.

One, Two, Buy Velcro Shoes: What Greg Taught Me

BARRY LANE

To all those aides who know why Ed
is so Special

His arms would stiffen like two-by-fours at his side. His face would distort into a grotesque mask as if he were being poked with hot irons. His eyes would close tight in horror, "She's comin' back!" he'd shout, patting his chest like a penitent as his whole body recoiled in terror. "It's all right, Greg," another voice inside him would reply. "She's gone, Greg." Greg was about to tie his shoe, and each time I tried to teach him he turned into a B-movie monster.

I was Greg's personal care attendant, which was another way of saying I was the guy who was supposed to follow Greg around and try to teach him something, which was another way of saying I was the interpreter of Greg's cryptic messages, which was another way of saying I was the guy who cleaned up Greg's messes.

Greg was a sixteen-year-old boy with autism being schooled at a private school for the retarded in the early 1980s, when such institutions were still politically correct in New Hampshire. They even still used the word *retarded* then, though two years later the move to *developmentally disabled* gained prominence. Labels are an institution's way of saying, Don't I know you from somewhere? and Greg was one to defy all labels; though *autism,* a term created by psychologist Leo Kanner in the 1950s to describe fourteen characteristics exhibited by schizophrenics, seemed to fit him fairly well.

He was about five feet tall with straight black hair that stuck up in several directions. He walked on his toes (one of Kanner's signs) and clucked often. Children with autism also often exhibit self-abusive behaviors, which in Greg's case involved walking along brick walls with the right side of his face pressed against the brick. He had stopped most of this activity by the time I met him, though the scabs and scars were still there. Some people with autism are savants like Dustin Hoffman's character in the movie *Rain Man,* but Greg's afflictions involved various types of other brain damage, which

3

meant he had little of what we might call normal speech. He did a lot of parroting. ("Go in the house, Greg?" I'd say. Greg's reply, "Go in the house.") In his file the label *severe and profound* was used to describe Greg's problem. This seemed to me the most apt and fitting description of Greg I had seen. One look in his eyes and you saw the severity of his pain, and the more I got to know Greg the more I became aware of just how profound a human being he was.

Greg will learn to tie his shoe with minimal assistance. This was the sentence that tormented my life. It was written in Greg's IEP, which stands for Independent Educational Plan, but because of that line I started referring to it as Greg's ITP or Independent Torture Plan. Goals like *Greg will undo the twist tie on a loaf of bread* or *Greg will make himself chocolate milk and drink it* were easy. Even goals like *Greg will learn to shave his face without losing the eyebrows* were not too difficult to master. But this tying-the-shoes thing got the worst of him every time we tried it.

First let me explain that the way they tied shoes at this school was different from the way you or I learned to tie shoes. I remember learning from Gary Fagan, an older boy in the neighborhood, when I was four. I remember how proud I was when I showed my mother. It was the "through the loop" stage that made the breakthrough for me. I can still remember how it felt when I pushed the loop through and almost magically the laces formed a bow. I remember quickly undoing it to see if it was luck or if I could repeat my success, and when I did it again and again I could feel a swelling sense of pride. Contrary to my own popular belief, I was educable, knowledge would stick to me, and I could demonstrate this for years by tying my shoe.

To teach Greg this daring feat, I was asked to break it down into several stages. These stages are, of course, etched in my memory like the Doublemint Gum jingles of my childhood:

> *Left hand: cross drop.*
> *Right hand: cross drop.*
> *Left hand*
> *under the triangle.*
> *Take both ends and*
> *pull tight.*
> *(repeat)*
> *Take both ends and*
> *pull*
> *but leave a little hole.*
> *Left through the hole*
> *going away from you.*
> *Right through the hole*
> *going toward you.*
> *Pinch both loops and*
> *Pull tight.*

Most days we couldn't get past the first two stages without Greg having a major tantrum. One day he ripped a shower curtain right off the rod in a Brando-like moment of utter contempt and outrage. It was after that hair-raising experience that I decided tying the shoe might not be quite as important as understanding what was happening inside Greg when he tried.

I began studying more about autism and I learned some startling facts. Because children with autism are left-brain deficient, they have great difficulty conceptualizing time with words. Most of us know today is today and tomorrow is tomorrow. We think, It's 8:00 A.M. now, I will finish breakfast and go to the store to buy milk at 8:30. Many people with autism can't have that thought because it requires an abstract concept of time. In other words, the only way a kid like Greg can structure time is in the present with ingrained routines and rituals that give him the same sense of order that we construct in thought. I remember reading a story in which a mother of a seven-year-old boy with autism described a major tantrum her son had on the way to school. She thought the routine was no different from any other day until she remembered she had passed a car that day. When you depend on external routines for mental clarity, just about any inevitable variation becomes an Orwellian assault on your thoughts.

That's when I started thinking seriously about the deeper implications of being Greg. If you had no way of creating time in your head, there was nothing to say that the past was past. The expression "Time is the great healer of all wounds" would not be true, because everything that had ever happened to you would continually happen to you in each moment of your waking life. There would be no past to escape, no future to hide in. If all humanity were like Greg, we would live the eternal return. We wouldn't have the luxury of saying, World War II happened before we were born; it would be happening right now, and we would be powerless to stop the painful thoughts unless we could be distracted by the present long enough to engage in some activity like stirring Hershey's syrup into a glass of milk. The pain trapped in Greg's gentle face suddenly began to make sense.

I began to pay closer attention to Greg's words when he had his tantrums. "She's comin' back," he'd say, his face contorted in excruciating pain. I asked Greg, "Who is she?" and Greg would reply, "Who's she?" his face still twisted with pain. The other most consistent voice was one that said, "It's all right, Greg, calm down." This was not a consoling voice but more a self-annihilating one. "Who's saying that?" I asked. "Who's saying that?" Greg parroted again. I realized this was getting us nowhere when Greg started saying my questions as part of his repertoire. I was just adding another disembodied voice to the confusion.

Then I began to investigate Greg's past. The social worker had told me a little about Greg's family. They were Portuguese, a big Catholic family. They loved each other but expressed it by shouting insults and hitting and calling up guilt. They had refused most respite care and Greg's younger brothers took care of him to fill in for his older brother who had recently left home to join the service. They had little money but were not poor in spirit. Just in passing she told me that Greg's maternal grandmother had taken him alone for summers when he was a young child. She had taught him to speak but died suddenly when he was five.

A month later I interviewed Greg's mother about his grandmother. I had gotten to know her well through the summer program I designed for Greg at his house. In her words, "Greg wouldn't speak for anyone but his Nana." His Nana took him for the summer when he was three and taught him to play peekaboo. She nurtured him and loved him so hard, he would pine away when she brought him back home in August to his big confusing family. Nana's sudden death of a stroke at fifty years old was a shock to everybody. On the way to the funeral Greg's mother and dad had stopped at Nana's house to get something. Greg was with them and bolted out of the car and into the house in front of them. He started looking for Nana in closets, in drawers, under beds. He kept shouting, "Peekaboo Nana, Nana Peekaboo." Greg's mother was greatly distressed and kept telling her husband, "That kid. That kid. Do something about that kid." Her husband finally grabbed young Greg by the shoulders, sat him down on Nana's bed, and in a stern voice said, "SHE'S GONE, GREG! ALL GONE! NO MORE! SHE'S NEVER COMING BACK!" Greg's mother described her son's reaction, "His head tipped over, his eyes closed, and he didn't speak again for eight years."

After hearing that story it was clear where Greg's tantrums came from. With no concept of time how could five-year-old Greg process grief? You or I would be able to reflect on a painful memory as something buried years in the past. For Greg, ten years ago was today waiting to happen over and over. A trigger as simple as tying a shoe would propel that moment into the present. Since Greg was four or five when he lived with his Nana, I could only speculate that, like me, that was the year he was learning to tie his shoes.

The next time Greg went to tie his shoe I put my theory to work. "Cross drop," I said, initiating the painful process. Greg's arms turned to timber and his head recoiled in that twisted mask of sadness. "She's comin back," he muttered as his eyes squeezed shut. "Greg," I said, "she loves you." I will always remember the moment that followed. Greg's entire body seemed to deflate as though an icy wind had stopped blowing and a warm sun was now shining over him. "She loves you," I said again. And this time his eyes opened wider than I'd ever seen and he turned to me, and with the wonder of a small child said, "She loves you, Greg."

No, Greg never learned to tie his shoe, and it was about a month later that I gave up and bought a pair of gray running shoes with Velcro fasteners with my own money. I confess I did not follow Greg's IEP with the same zeal after that day. Greg taught me that the forest was not the sum of the trees but something larger and far more magnificent than I ever imagined possible. My IEP has not been the same since.

You Can't Always Judge a New Book by Its Cover

KIMBERLY CAMPBELL

Sporting cowboy hats, six senior boys re-created an important scene from Craig Lesley's book *Winterkill*. The video was high quality: no laughing, dialog could be heard, all the group members participated in the video. The scene brought the book, specifically its characters, to life for those in the class who had read a different novel. This was everything I had hoped for when creating this literary circle project as part of reading workshop.

As the video faded to blue, I asked my first question, "How does this scene compare with the fight scene at the end of the book?" Silence. Blank looks were all I saw on the faces of these six high school seniors who were "experts" on this book—this book they'd spent six weeks reading and discussing every Wednesday in class. I tried a second question about the death of a key character. Again, no response. So, I addressed my third question to a group member. "David, what can you tell me about Red Shirt?"

"Um, I guess I must have skimmed that part?"

"That part? We're talking about the last half of the book!"

"Yeah, um, that's the part I skimmed."

Knowing nods and nervous laughter from the other group members were offered up as support for poor David.

I continued to ask questions, working my way back through the book. No answers indicated any real comprehension of this book past chapter eight or nine. I was shocked, disappointed. The high-quality video was a ruse, a flashy project intended to "wow" so that I wouldn't notice they hadn't really read—or at least finished reading.

Great, the first group and we were off to a dismal start. No worries; I knew the other groups would rise to my expectations. So I turned my attention to holding this group accountable.

"Gentleman, when completing your self-evaluations of this project, please address this issue of failing to complete the book. Think about it in terms of the objectives of literary circles—to have time to talk about a book with others who are reading it. To enjoy real talk about real books—to become lifelong readers. Second, address the issue from the perspective of academic dishonesty.

"Next group, please."

"Yeah, we read *Ordinary People*. And, like this guy, named Conrad, was all freaking out about his brother who died. And was real depressed and stuff. I'd say if you like boring books, read this. I could hardly, like, understand it."

The rest of the group echoed this tone. No compassion for Conrad or his family. I asked, "How would you define Conrad's world—his culture?"

"I don't know."

"Is his culture like yours here in Estacada [a small rural community]?"

"I guess not. I think they were rich and stuff."

"Did you feel any sympathy for Conrad? Did you feel any anger about his mother at all?"

"Not really."

I looked at the category of empathy on my scoring rubric. Great!

"Any questions from the class?"

Of course not. Why would any of them care enough to ask about a boring book about a depressed rich kid!

The next group was delightful. They brought *The Bean Trees* to life. Their video was of much poorer quality—too much giggling and nauseating camera work. But as they talked about the book, their genuine enthusiasm was contagious. We were back on track—I hoped on a roll.

No such luck unfortunately.

Group four went to the front, minus two group members who informed me that they had not read the book and thus there was no point in their participating. The other three group members held up a poster of the book and set a painstakingly crafted replica of the family home on the desk.

"Well, our presentation is going to be pretty half-assed because most of us didn't finish the book. It was just about some girl and her family and how they got left by their mother, and so they just kept walking around."

What does one say in response? I did comment on rethinking their choice of phrasing and then attempted to salvage this group by focusing on the crestfallen girl who had made the replica of the house. I asked her a few questions, which she answered, but in a quiet, just-let-me-sit-down voice.

And then it was over, finally. The longest eighty-seven-minute period of my life. I sat for several moments in my chair, the same questions swirling over and over in my head: What just happened? How did I fail to convey that the purpose of these presentations was to bring these books to life so that others would want to read them? That these groups were to deepen the reading experience because there would be time to talk? That I had trusted them to be self-directed readers/learners? Why did they let me down?

At lunch I sat silently, staring at my yogurt.

"Bad day?" asked a colleague.

"It's one of those days when I wonder why I'm even here! What made me think I could make readers out of them."

I don't remember if my colleague responded. It didn't really matter. I grew angrier as I relived each project. On my drive home, I was still brooding. During dinner preparations phrases replayed over and over:

"Boring."

"Total wimp."

"Who cares?"

"Guess I skimmed that part."

"It's okay, if you like a book with no action and a bunch of boring characters."

As I prepared for bed, my focus shifted from that of angry teacher who had been let down by unmotivated students to angry but curious teacher-researcher who wanted to know what I could learn—what they could learn—from this. I went back over the layout of the literary circles. Went back to the first day I had introduced this idea . . .

I had begun by sharing my frustration in previous years that students were not sharing their reading—that group talks never went beyond the surface because students were all reading different books. I shared my own discovery of reading a book with a small group and having time to discuss what I had read. I told them about book groups made up of teachers on the Estacada staff.

Excitedly, I showed them the choice of novels. With the exception of one title, *Ordinary People,* they were all brand-new books—never been opened. I inhaled the new-book smell and encouraged them to do the same. I joyously told them just a little bit about each title and then asked them to come pick the book that sounded best to them. I had just enough copies for each student to have one book.

Some students ran to the table and grabbed a stack of books, which they then distributed to friends; most picked the books by sheer number of copies rather than interest. Others reluctantly reached for a title. No one picked up several books and skimmed. No one made any effort to inhale the new-book smell. They chatted about everything but books until I required that they sit and read. (Perhaps I should have addressed these observations, but I didn't. I was sure my ideas would work once they got into reading.)

I asked students to read for ten to fifteen minutes and then to meet with their fellow readers to talk. Afterward they were to write to me about the books they had chosen:

Why this selection?

Initial reaction?

What, if anything, confuses you?

What strikes you?

What predictions do you make?

The *Winterkill* group (the group that went on to create the mostly-flash-little-substance video) wrote that their selection was based on the fact that this was the "only good one left." Another group wrote, "It was the last one." Of course there were groups that selected for "literary" reasons: "It sounded good." "It was the only one that sounded suspenseful." Even these groups, however, were relying on my assessment of these books—my sales pitch. I've often been disappointed by books that came highly recommended to me. Why did I assume they would share my tastes?

Looking back, I wonder why I didn't allow more than one group to read the same book. Why did I insist on having just enough books, which forced kids to settle for what was left? Why did I pick the titles that were available? Why did I assume they would want to read these books? Why did I assume they even needed to talk in depth about reading?

I went back and reread the discussion notes that I had required at the end of each Wednesday discussion session. I realized these notes were not an actual reflection of what was happening. For example, the *Winterkill* group, the ones who skimmed the last half of the book, wrote, "We feel the book becomes interesting and intensely evolving and we cannot put it down." (I know, they told me what I wanted to hear and I saw what I wanted to see.) The clues were there but I had overlooked them in an effort to hold on to my great idea. I had valued the idea of literary circles over the actual practice. I had stopped looking at my students as individual readers and looked instead at refining the assignment so that students would be able to meet my high expectations. And I was the one who decided they needed empathy for these characters. That it was essential that they "like" the book. Maybe they had preferred to be self-directed learners—learners who went in their own direction, not the direction I had so carefully laid out for them.

I shared these observations and frustrations with the class the next day. I then asked them to write for me the story of their group presentations and what they had learned from this whole experience. As I read through these stories, I saw real readers. One commented that he had learned he needed quiet to read. Another shared that she was struggling to understand the book and had found rereading very helpful. Bill commented on ways the ending of the novel he had read could have been rewritten. Tony wrote that he felt more confident about his reading "skills."

And, they had suggestions for me, too:

Provide more copies of each title so that choices are really based on interest rather than what's left.

Be more specific regarding project expectations—even model one.

Build in more accountability for the reading—don't allow us to be uncommitted.

Remember that we don't all love reading like you do.

I did try literary circles again, with two new classes, second semester. I shared with them the story of my failure first semester and what those students—those readers—had taught me. I incorporated the suggestions they had so generously shared with me. As a result, I had several groups choose to read the same book, and it was wonderful to sit back during these presentations and watch the "experts" question each other (I suspect they read more carefully in anticipation of questioning by their peers). I also directed written responses at the beginning of some literary circle sessions to get a sense of where each reader was in his or her own comprehension of the book—and to send my students a message that they needed to be caught up on the reading but that there was also time to get help from peers in the group and from me. (Please note that the schedule for reading each book was designed by each group.) I handed out a sample scoring guide weeks before the final project was due and we negotiated the criteria for evaluation. We brainstormed project ideas as a class, and I did a miniproject on a book I was reading. I checked in more with groups regarding their project—and each group submitted a tentative lesson plan three weeks before the due date.

The results were much higher quality presentations—quality as defined by the entire community of readers, not just me. And a much more positive attitude toward reading came through as each group brought their book to life. I now have a *Great Gatsby* party experience, complete with Snickers bar appetizers; a game of *Huckleberry Finn* in which each player is given a hand-crafted miniature raft and asked to relive the plot highlights of the book; and a talk show interview with characters from *Pigs in Heaven*—examples of what kids can do when they connect with a book as a group.

I've learned to let kids switch books within the first two weeks and to step in as a mediator if the group feels a member isn't committed. I've learned to both let go and take control. I've found myself trusting my gut while paying close attention to what is happening throughout the literary circle process. I've learned to ask, How's it going with your book? Your group? I've learned to stop and investigate when I find myself feeling perplexed rather than just forging ahead, trying to force my ideas to work. So, they may not all love reading the way I do, but they are all readers. I know this now; so do they.

References

Cody, R. 1994. *Ricochet River.* Hillsboro, OR: Blue Heron.

Fitzgerald, F. S. 1993. *The Great Gatsby.* New York: Macmillan.

Guest, J. 1976. *Ordinary People.* New York: Random House.

Kingsolver, B. 1988. *The Bean Trees.* New York: HarperCollins.

———. 1993. *Pigs in Heaven.* New York: HarperCollins.

Lesley, C. 1984. *Winterkill*. New York: Dell.

O'Brien, T. 1990. *The Things They Carried*. New York: Penguin.

Twain, M. 1973. *The Adventures of Huckleberry Finn*. New York: Simon & Schuster.

Motivating Alison with a Challenge: A Tale of Two Students

HERMAN G. WELLER

A t noon each day, from the windows of my classroom on the third floor, I watched a disheartening example of what adults can make children do in the name of educational efficiency. Out of our huge, gray stone high school building hurried 1700 juniors and seniors with their complement of teachers, most wearing their new fall jackets and sweaters. They were rapidly replaced by 1700 first-year students and sophomores with their teachers. The only thing missing in the cool air of October 1968 was a factory whistle during the change between double sessions. All but one of the school's students were African American; the football coach's daughter was white. Half of the faculty was African American; half was white. Directly across the highway from our muddy football field, we could see the grassy turf of a beautiful high school that didn't have double-session classes. I was a new teacher who was struggling to construct mathematics lessons that would allow the students more than fleeting opportunities for learning during the allotted forty-two-minute class periods.

After a two-year absence from the United States, I was perceiving America with new senses. I had returned during the summer from two years of teaching mathematics and science in a West African boarding school just south of the Sahara Desert. In northern Ghana on a busy day, perhaps ten vehicles had raised billows of red dust on the laterite highway past the school. In America that fall all my senses were nearly overwhelmed by the hurry and flurry of the inner city of this giant northeastern metropolis! In addition, I was still adjusting to a multitude of national tragedies that had taken place in the United States while I was away, tragedies that my tenth-grade students never discussed in the presence of this tall, skinny, white ex–Peace Corps volunteer. On some autumn days I just wanted to scream, Please earth, stop rotating so quickly into the future! Let us all rest a few moments and get our wits together! In my absence, Robert F. Kennedy and Martin Luther King, Jr., had been assassinated; large portions of Detroit, Newark, and Chicago had been looted and burned; and more than thirty other cities had suffered similar violence.

The music permeating this huge city seemed almost too rich and insistent for my ears. In northern Ghana I had usually fallen asleep to sounds of traditional drumming at a nearby compound, while on the national radio E. T. Mensah's high-life band had made mellow sounds or Fats Domino had "twisted again." In America, the vibrant energy of the voices of James Brown, Aretha Franklin, the Temptations, Marvin Gay, and Tammy Terrell poured out all day long into the inner-city streets from store doorways, row-house porches, and the windows of passing cars. Small groups of young men hoping to be "discovered" would practice harmony on street corners and, occasionally, in the boys restroom that abutted my classroom. When the nicely blended sounds wafted into the back of my classroom during a geometry lesson, I would fight back a smile, put down my chalk, and hurry out through the hallway to the lavatory to ask the young men to practice elsewhere.

In northern Ghana's savannah, I had grown accustomed to seeing miles of green fields of ripening millet corn or tall elephant grass edged by giant baobab trees. In this American city's streets, my eyes were assaulted everywhere by colorful designs of graffiti upon graffiti on walls and signs—names, logos, and gang names. The creators of this street art had obviously spent many hours practicing with chalk and spray paint to perfect their individual styles. There was only a small amount of graffiti on the outside of our high school building, and none in the interior.

Teaching at this American city school did not resemble the mental picture I had formed of it the year before in Accra, Ghana, when the American recruiter had spoken to Peace Corps volunteers during our annual medical checkup. Instead of the highly motivated students I had left at the school in northern Ghana, I was now faced with Alison, Henry, and other inner-city students, many of whom did not seem to place a very high priority on succeeding in high school. In Ghana the industriousness of all my students had led me to believe that I was becoming an accomplished teacher, a teacher who would certainly become an instant success in America. In the United States I found that I was almost totally lacking in an essential component of the good teacher—the ability to motivate students who were very suspicious of school's value.

But at least I had formulated the Clever Plan for the transformation of Alison's lackluster geometry learning and the elimination of Henry's boredom in general math class. I taught Alison's tenth-grade geometry class as I taught all my mathematics classes—with lecture and discussion while the students sat at near-attention in straight rows. That is how I had been taught as I grew up, from kindergarten through university. The ten students who tried very hard sat in the first row or two of desks; the twenty students who tried less hard sat farther back. Alison sat in the second row. She was occasionally animated, usually in conversations with her nearby girlfriends. She seemed not to let geometry impinge too intensely upon her life. She was maintaining a grade average somewhere between a D+ and a C−.

In my second-period general mathematics class, Henry, whom I had not been able to persuade to take geometry, sat alone in the back near the windows. He invariably did all the problems perfectly, and probably to keep from being bored, he practiced his personal graffiti-style lettering and graphics on the desktop or notebook paper. Henry was not willing to risk doing poorly in geometry class. He had an A+ average doing the same general math problems he had probably done since seventh grade.

After school every day, I rode the subway to my apartment near a local university. This public conveyance squealed and rumbled directly below my apartment house every fifteen minutes, its passage each time being marked by a tiny plume of brick dust emerging from the apartment's window frames. One day coming home in the subway, I was hanging onto a pole, and nearby, Alison and some of her girlfriends clung to other poles. I noticed that she was holding the geometry book and several other books in her arms. So I initiated the Clever Plan. I said, How you doin'? and made a few lame jokes about why she was carrying her geometry book home: To use it as a paperweight? A hammer?

Alison reacted the way I had hoped she would. She took my challenge on the spot. She said that she could do as well in geometry as anyone else in the class. In turn, she challenged me. She asked me what I would do if she got an A on the next geometry quiz. I suspected that there was little chance of that happening. After getting a C− and worse on the previous quizzes, how could she have enough geometry skills to earn an A on new material? I told Alison that if she got an A on the next quiz, I would scream an announcement to the class that she had gotten an A, and I would also hang up a poster in front of the class proclaiming the wonderful event. She said okay. The first part of the Clever Motivator's plan was in place.

The next day, I began to be amazed at the success of the first part of the Clever Plan. For the next two weeks, Alison never let a new geometric concept, principle, or technique pass until she was certain that she had mastered it. Every geometry period she resolutely kept her hand up, asking questions until she was satisfied that she understood everything. Her homework performance improved steadily.

I set the second part of the Clever Plan in motion on Monday of the second week of the Transformed Alison. In general math class during study time, Henry finished his classwork problems quickly and fell to practicing his graffiti lettering skills on scrap paper. I found a few moments to stop by Henry's desk, comment favorably on his artistic talent, and suggest a possible business deal: if I gave him poster board and several magic markers, would he construct a poster announcing that certain students had earned A grades on the geometry quiz? Henry agreed in principle.

In geometry, the students took a quiz that Thursday. The Clever Motivator was somewhat apprehensive. The proof of my motivational pudding would be in Alison's geometric proving. I was honestly astounded! Alison earned an A− on the quiz. Only four other students earned A or A− grades in my two geometry classes! The Clever Motivator's plan was working! On Friday in general mathematics, I negotiated a graphics contract with Henry. His commission for the work? He would keep the felt-tipped markers as payment. We shook hands on it, and Henry left for the weekend with the markers and poster board.

On Monday during general mathematics class, Henry brought a neatly lettered poster—blue, red, and green on white—proclaiming the names of students who had earned A's and A−'s on the geometry quiz. Exactly what I had hoped for! I congratulated Henry on his work and told him that our business deal was completed. The felt-tipped markers were his. I hung the poster in the classroom above the chalkboard behind my desk. Would this Clever Plan not somehow result in a Motivated Henry who would feel more a part of the mathematics classes and perhaps even wish to take an exciting class like geometry?

In third-period geometry came the Motivational Moment. After I took roll, I called the class's attention to the poster at the front of the room, commended Henry's graphics design, and announced that I had promised Alison that if she earned an A on a quiz, I would scream to the class that she had done it. I proceeded to scream to the class that she had earned an A. Alison's reaction was one of satisfaction. Then I passed back the quizzes and discussed them with the students.

In television sitcoms or paperback teacher-biographies, these Clever Strategies would probably have changed Alison's math performance for at least the remainder of the school year and possibly even put her on the road to becoming a scientist or engineer. They probably would have changed Henry's life, also. He might have decided that geometry was the fun class for him and stopped wasting his time doing mathematics that he already knew inside out. Or he might have taken the felt-tipped markers and start perfecting a new postmodern visual art genre. Visions of possibilities for Alison and Henry passed through this neophyte teacher's imagination.

And what did actually happen to the Transformed Alison and the Motivated Henry?

From that time on, a Transformed Alison earned a steady C in geometry, a slight improvement in her previous performance. My continued efforts to motivate her further had little apparent effect. Walking to class the following week, I noticed some graffiti—blue, red, and green on white—on the hall wall several doors down from my classroom. It was a gang name in a very familiar graffiti style. Where had I seen that style before? On a street corner near my house? On a sign in the subway tunnels? Oh, no! It was the style that Henry had practiced repeatedly in my general math class. So that was the use to which Henry was putting the Motivational Markers! The next day, I confronted Henry in class. I asked him what he was going to do about the graffiti on the hallway wall before I reported his unique graffiti style to the principal's office. I supplied him with cleaning materials and the graffiti disappeared from the walls before any official trouble could befall him.

What did this neophyte teacher learn from "touching the lives" of Alison and Henry? I learned that teaching is neither a sitcom nor a paperback novel. Students' lives are far more difficult to influence than I had thought. The teacher was certainly not the only influence in the lives of these young people. They had developed their values through many years during which success in school had provided little payoff for many of them or, worse, had provided negative payoff. Perhaps somewhere in America the aims of some future scientists and engineers might be sparked by the celebration of success on one geometry quiz or by the recognition of graphic talent by a wise pedagogue. I realized then that students' goals would not be influenced so easily by this ex–Peace Corps teacher.

However, since the time of the Clever Plan I have never stopped trying to provide those motivational sparks for my students. In some mysterious reflexive way, the Clever Plan seems to have worked on me.

Passing and Failing

AMBER DAHLIN

Passing problems along is unethical, right? Passing students to ensure that you won't see them again is wrong, isn't it? But sometimes (at least I thought so then) it's better to send trouble on its way, not invite it in for dinner or a research paper. So when I had a suspected murderer/child molester in a research-writing course several years ago, I practiced every avoidance strategy at my command, and then I sent the man on his way with a D. His passing illuminates my failing.

I teach at Metropolitan State College in Denver, an urban undergraduate college with an eclectic student population of job-changers, recent high school graduates, and street-smart radicals. During the first week of class, which we spend getting to know one another, I am prepared to hear accounts of job worries, concerts, high school events, family troubles, an assortment of hobbies, and complaints about education in general. John went to another level entirely.

As we went through the circle of introductions, John stated, with an air of mystery, that he was in a "serious political situation." Other students, their curiosity piqued, of course asked what he meant. He was referring to the molestation and murder of a six-year-old boy on a bike path in Denver. John was under susupicion for the crime. He said that he and his roommate were being harrassed by the police, after having been questioned several times. While answering inquiries about what one student called "that astounding murder thing," John maintained an aura of nonchalance, seeming to enjoy the notoriety of being a murder suspect.

I should explain my own reactions at this point. Child abuse, domestic violence, sexual abuse—these topics literally make me cry. I was depressed to be reminded of the boy's murder, which had caused a tumult in the city. Why, I wondered, would a person bring this incident up during a round of casual introductions?

Furthermore, I was raised in Wyoming, where teachers were like ranchers and students were the cattle; where if you had problems you handled them yourself, in stoic silence; where dirty little secrets were supposed to stay put in prairie dog holes. When John finished his introduction my instinct was to say, We just don't *talk* about those things. And we moved on (sort of like, Oh, Sandy likes to snowboard and John is a murder suspect. Next?).

Internally, though, my thoughts stampeded. Did he really do it? Was he actually an eccentric victim himself, hassled by the police? If he had done it, why would he bring it up here? If he hadn't, why would he bring it up here? How was I supposed to react? Was I in danger? Was the rest of the class in danger? I decided to believe his version—that he was indeed being hassled by the police. I was relieved, though, when he didn't attend class much. His writing skills were adequate in the work he did turn in. At midterm he had a D.

Right after that, I held conferences to discuss each student's major research project for the rest of the semester. I dreaded John's conference. I didn't want to be alone with him. Here is how it went:

ME: Hi, John. What topic are you thinking about?

JOHN: Computers.

ME: *(That seems safe enough)* I see. What exactly about computers are you interested in?

JOHN: I want to create a computer program that can hypnotize people.

ME: *(What?)* Hmm.

JOHN: Yeah, see, people would get into the program and you'd be able to hypnotize people and control their thoughts.

ME: *(This is sick)* Is such a thing actually possible?

JOHN: Yeah, I've found some stuff on it already.

ME: Oh.

JOHN: And I'd call it Computerized-Hypnosis-Inducing-Learning-Device. C.H.I.L.D.

ME: *(Oh, no! That acronym! He did do it. He is a child molester. I'm going to throw up)* Oh.

And then he left, with me having said nothing of substance. I didn't express the revulsion I felt. I never said, John, this topic makes me think you're seriously disturbed. Or, John, I'm going to recommend that you see a counselor. Or, What is the *matter* with you? I felt an overwhelming urge to flee, simply to be a hundred miles away from this horrible person who even if he hadn't murdered a child was definitely sick. After he left I sat in my office and thought, I hate this place, I hate this place, I hate this place.

Looking back, I can analyze this gut-level reaction and play out the options. I have always avoided conflict and confrontation, partially from upbringing and partially from personal preference. Realistically, what can a writing teacher do about a murderer? If everyone did as I did, though, let

John pass through without even acknowledging there was something wrong, then he would go blithely through life doing whatever he wanted. Yet if I had confronted John, told him he was sick, he might have flown at me in a rage, started sending me threatening letters, stalked me at school.

I know that I failed as a teacher because I did not teach John. I didn't want to teach him—I wanted him to disappear. I avoided him as much as possible throughout the semester, I gave shallow responses to his writing, and I pretended that everything was normal when clearly it was not. John, I am certain, learned nothing about research or writing in that class.

Part of my uncertainty in dealing with this student was a result of feeling isolated myself, a new faculty member who had not yet established a support system. That semester was my first at an urban institution, where, frankly, there is greater likelihood of running into disturbed people. My naïveté and inexperience were contributing factors, and I hope that if a similar situation occurred now I would call upon more resources, both personal and institutional.

Yet I am haunted. I did not act as a responsible human being. I wonder if my inability to confront John somehow contributed to his continued illness. John was not convicted of the murder, but I wonder where he is. I'm afraid I'll see a computerized hypnosis program in a catalog someday or read his name in the newspaper in connection with another murder.

I wish I could say that a realization of my own culpability came in time to matter, but it didn't. John never came back to class. I got a phone call from him at the end of the semester. He wondered if there was any way he could make up his absences or take an incomplete. I thought, If I fail him he might register for my session again. He might find out that I have a seven-year-old daughter and come after her. Rationally I know that this was unlikely, but at the time it seemed possible.

I thought, If I pass him I'll never see him again.

But I was wrong. He is still here with me.

Omniscience 301

SUSAN OHANIAN

I really feel tired today," Jean told me as she walked into the classroom. She flopped into a chair with a huge sigh. "We were up all night waiting for my sister's babies to be born."

"Babies with an *s?*" I asked.

"Yep. Twins," smiled Jean. "Two girls."

"That must be exciting," I said. Being as intrigued as the next person by multiple births, I wasn't just being polite. I sat down across the table from Jean, inviting her to tell more.

"My mother is really excited. They are her first grandchildren." Jean paused and then added, matter-of-factly, "My sister isn't married, but she has a boyfriend and they're gonna get married when he gets a job." She straightened up a bit, seeming to gain a burst of energy. "All of us kids went to the hospital and waited. My father bought us cokes and hamburgers in the coffee shop. We had to wait until four o'clock in the morning for those babies to be born."

"No wonder you're tired," I said. I asked about the babies' names, hair color, and so on. Over the next few months I heard a lot about those babies. Jean usually had a baby anecdote as she came into the classroom, and I arranged for her to do a research project on facts about twins to receive extra credit in science. Jean became very knowledgeable about twins in fact and fiction; so did everybody else in the class.

In our daily note exchange Jean wrote a lot about the twins, filling me in on how much they slept, what they ate, which one was cranky. She wrote a very funny note about how much trouble she had getting food into their mouths and not all over them—and her. Jean wrote about rushing home from school to take the babies for walks, about staying up very late baby-sitting. After a few months the twins became a frequent excuse for missed homework, for poor spelling test scores, for inability to concentrate on class assignments.

I began to worry that Jean was being worn down by too much responsibility. She was, after all, just twelve years old herself, and she had a right to her own childhood.

The day Jean came back to school from a four-day absence and told me she'd been out because she had to take care of the twins, I made no comment to her, but I knew I had to act. Over several months I'd been listening to Jean tell me about the babies' mother's failure to assume responsibility:

"My mom is kind of mad 'cause my sister never stays home to take care of the babies. She wants to party. My sister says she's only sixteen and she's too young to be an old lady yet. Her friends party and she wants to party too."

"My mom is afraid she'll get fired if she misses any more work. And my dad just isn't any good with babies. I'm the only one who can do it."

During my planning period I rushed to the guidance office. "I know people have their problems," I said to the counselor, not bothering with any preliminary Hello, how are you? "But Jean is a child. She needs to be in school. She has the *right* to be in school. I don't know what her parents can be thinking of. Jean has ability. If the adults in that family could exert a little responsibility, she wouldn't be failing half her subjects. But if her mother continues to keep her out of school to baby-sit the twins, Jean will end up being a dropout and an unwed mother. Just like her sister."

All this came out in a rush of frustration. When I finally paused to take a breath, the guidance counselor managed to get in a question, "What twins?"

"Her sister's kids." I felt a bit smug. Our school was like all others I've ever known—either firsthand or from distant colleagues—operating in a structure that guaranteed animosity between teachers and guidance counselors. Teachers, after all, have the hard work; we have these hordes of restless, turned-off adolescents over whom we are expected to exercise every manner of beneficent influence (moral, health, consumer, citizenship) while at the same time teaching them to read, write, divide fractions, memorize General Washington's battle plans, and treat one another with decency. Guidance counselors are set up to be the pals of individual students who wander into their offices.

Now there's a perfect example of inequity right there: Where are the offices for teachers? A counselor has an office, a telephone, and ready access to a secretary. A counselor can go to the bathroom when she wants; a counselor can get someone else to file her papers. A seventh-grade teacher tends to the needs of twenty-five adolescents at a time; a counselor lends a sympathetic ear to individual children at her convenience—by appointment. A teacher assigns homework; a counselor hands out jelly beans. If Johnny complains, the counselor appears at the teacher's door, asking, What seems to be your problem? Teachers think counselors learn the necessary supercilious intonation for that question in a course called Have You Stopped Beating Your Students?

I knew such judgments were unfair, that just thinking about counselors turned me into a whiner, but still, at that moment I savored the knowledge that Jean had favored me with inside information, information the guidance counselor, who had long ago crowned herself Princess Pal, wasn't privy to. I enjoyed letting this woman know that a regular old language arts teacher, one traditional enough to insist on homework and spelling tests, was Jean's confidante. And so I laid on the detail. "They must be about six months old by now—Jane and Joan. They all live with Jean's parents—the mother and the babies. And it sounds as though all the kids stay up half the night—with Jean in charge." I paused a second and then added, "Can you imagine leaving Jean in charge?"

"Jean doesn't have a sister." The counselor's calm, confident voice was a bucket of ice water on my fiery excitement. "She's an only child."

"She can't be!" I insisted.

"She's in here a lot," said the counselor. "I'm sure I'd know if she had siblings." The counselor did not say this smugly—merely with a lot of confidence. She was very sure of herself and her information. But then, counselors are always very sure of themselves, always certain that they know best how to watch over the concerns of the children in our care. It's another required course: How to Avoid Revealing Any Smidgen of Insecurity in Front of Teachers. Otherwise known as Omniscience 301.

I kept repeating, "I don't believe it." Not only did I know all about Sherry, Jean's older sister and mother of the twins, but there were also the three younger siblings. Jean was lackadaisical and sloppy about most school-work—starting many assignments but finishing few, losing the ones she did complete—but she was a devoted letter writer. Every day she wrote me a long, detailed note, and most days this note was about her family. Even before the twins were born, Jean had written funny family stories, recounting the antics of those three younger siblings, describing the mischief they got into, the fun they all had together. Jean wasn't vague in her notes: she described trips to the country to pick apples, being paid to paint the fence at their grandparents' house. Jean wrote about the card games her siblings enjoyed, the skating and sledding mishaps, the birthday parties, neighborhood baseball games, trips to the mall. I could recall a long, detailed list of the activities and adventures of Jean and her siblings.

The counselor pulled Jean's permanent file from the cabinet and there it was: Jean was an only child, no siblings. Right then and there, the counselor phoned Jean's mother, a homemaker who did not have a job outside the home. The counselor explained that the school was updating files and verifying information. Jean's mother confirmed that Jean was an only child. An imaginative only child, I suddenly realized, and one who must know more about twins than any other kid in the school. Hey, Jean probably knew more about twins than any adult in the school.

I was so fascinated by what Jean had pulled off that I didn't even think about eating humble pie in front of the counselor. I was especially fascinated by the fact that nobody squealed on Jean. Kids who lived on her street—right next door, in fact—didn't breathe a hint that there might be anything amiss in the stories she was spinning about the babies. As I looked back, I realized they hadn't paid much attention to Jean's and my enthusiasm for the twins. But seventh-grade communication with a teacher is often individual. Seventh graders interact with one another in packs—in the hallways and the cafeteria. Those who choose to talk to the teacher do so one at a time.

I wondered if race had anything to do with it. Most of the class was black. Jean was white. Were the twins Jean's way of making sure she got noticed? Black kids squealed on each other in minor ways all the time—accusing each other of cheating, of exaggerating, of just being full of it. Was there some sort of reverse code that prevented them from squealing on a white kid?

I'd never known seventh graders to be particularly loyal to one another simply because they were all seventh graders banding together against adults. If seventh graders didn't snitch as readily as third graders, they did, nonetheless, snitch. So why did they choose to keep silent about Jean's tall tales? Jean was an ordinary sort of child—neither particularly popular nor an outcast. She wasn't a good student, but neither was anybody else in my class. By helping her with her projects on twins, I'd helped her raise her marks in science and social studies, but that kind of help was available to any student in my class. Besides, neither Jean nor her classmates sustained any long-term interest in grades.

Every student in our language arts class, as well as most students in her other classes, must have known there were no siblings, no twins. Students saw Jean getting all that special attention from teachers—all those, How are the twins?—and they let it happen. They let it happen for eight months. And who knows? They might have let Jean's tales go on forever had I not stumbled across the truth. Maybe Jean's classmates figured she needed the fantasy. Live and let live: lie and let lie. Maybe I'm a coward, but I never confronted her with it. I just stopped asking about the twins, and she just stopped talking about them.

Her months of stringing me along forced me to take a good hard look at myself. I prided myself on being so savvy, someone with such a good feel for kids and their talk, so tuned in to their hopes, dreams, fears, longings . . . and lies. No teacher wants to think she actually sets herself up to be lied to, that she might encourage falsehoods. But faced with Jean's stories, I had to ask myself, Why me? Of her seven teachers, two principals, two guidance counselors, numerous librarians, aides, nurses, secretaries, custodians, and hall monitors, why did Jean choose me?

Why me? Is it my heart-on-my-sleeve sympathy and kindness? My enthusiastic ear? My willingness to drop formal lessons and capitalize on one child's particular interest of the moment? Or am I just more gullible than most? And more energetic? I mean, I didn't just listen to Jean's stories. I organized all those grand, across-the-curriculum study units. I prodded other teachers and the librarian to get involved. The science teacher, after all, did not know of the twins' existence until I suggested that Jean's research report might be worthy of science credit. And the science teacher never got involved in listening to stories of the twins as excuses for missed homework.

As I sit here looking at events backward, I can recognize two patterns: I rarely smelled a lie, and when I did I tried to deal with it sideways, never directly. I suspect this is true because I believe it's better to do nothing than to do something bad. As every teacher knows, when you teach you have no time to think. None. Kids are in your face, not sitting at your feet while you contemplate your navel or your guidebook. Every day, a teacher works with difficult children in difficult circumstances; she must decide if she has any business trying to peel away any of those layers of protective coating that these children wear. I, for one, never found that Omniscience 301 course in the catalog. All I can do is pick my own peas, try to deal with each day as it comes. I can't pretend there's ever been a master plan.

So that's the story. It started out as my contribution to this volume on teachers' admissions of failure. As I sat here, making a list of my classroom disasters, I had a tough time choosing: The time ninth graders bought ice cream sandwiches in the cafeteria and staged an ice cream war during my fifth-period English class? The time I left the building for the day, failing to notice that one of my third graders was asleep in the closet? The time the principal yelled at one of my students and I burst into tears? The September a student showed up for a week before I noticed he wasn't one of mine but rather an escapee from the class for the emotionally disturbed? The time I rigorously rehearsed eighth graders for a Christmas play that I adapted from a great story and then, in front of the whole school, they extemporized and gave it a whole new spin, one with a decidedly negative social value? The time I showed off the beautiful bouquet of flowers my most obstreperous student had presented to me and then two hours later his father came storming into the school looking for the twenty-dollar bill the kid had stolen?

Such stories are kind of fun, but in the end I rejected them because I realize that spectacular as they may be, they are just one-time events, trivial incidents never to be repeated and unlikely to reveal anything about the nature of teaching. As a teacher, I'm more interested in habits of mind, those attitudes that bespeak both my own unique teacherliness and some universal bond that ties me to colleagues everywhere. In telling Jean's story, I set out to tell about a failure, but then, somewhere in the telling, I decided that maybe it isn't a failure after all. As with most things of the classroom, the moral is a muddle. The Standardists will line up on one side and the Freedom Fighters on another. I tell the story with some chagrin, but if I admit that I'll probably behave the same way next time, then am I proclaiming myself an unrepentant failure? I ask myself how Jean's life would have been improved had I recognized the lie and can't come up with an answer. Being a teacher means confronting the dark ambiguity of not having clear landmarks of success and failure. Being a teacher means asking lots of questions and not finding many answers.

Fear, Incompetence, and Fraud

TOM ROMANO

The university had hired me primarily to teach English education courses and to supervise student teachers. I also taught writing courses where I was needed. Because I had written a young adult novel as part of my dissertation and had studied the writing processes of fiction writers, I taught fiction writing, too. In the spring of my first year, I was scheduled to teach advanced fiction writing, a veritable plum of a course. Smaller class size, upper-level, motivated students, many of them graduate students.

In the fall I had taught beginning fiction writing. That course of sophomores, juniors, and a sprinkling of seniors had gone well. Each week the students wrote or revised five pages of fiction, met with me for fifteen-minute conferences, and discussed their writing in peer groups. The students also read short stories by professional writers and Don Murray's *Shoptalk* (1990), a book in which Murray and hundreds of writers talk about various aspects of writing.

The prospect of teaching advanced fiction writing, however, daunted me. To be blunt, I was afraid. I was afraid of not being perceptive enough when reading students' manuscripts, afraid of not knowing enough when I conducted discussions, afraid of students who would know more than I and write better than I. I was afraid of fraud. You could tell that by the plans I made.

I ordered a thick, information-packed textbook, Janet Burroway's *Writing Fiction* (1992). Burroway would add rigor and subject matter to the course, I reasoned; she would offer students information about fiction writing that I didn't possess. Doubt in my own competence and my need for control in foreign territory drove me as I designed the syllabus in much the same way I had for beginning fiction writing: textbook assignments and response papers, weekly writing or revision of at least five pages of fiction, metacognitive one-pagers about that fiction, compilation of a learning portfolio, and weekly conferences with me and with peer response groups.

By the second week of the quarter much had gone awry. Cliques had formed, the most troublesome of which was a group of three undergraduates. The quality of talk often degenerated in workshops. My nondirective, inquiring conferencing style didn't work for many of the graduate students. One student told me that my conferencing style was a running joke among the graduate assistants on the fourth floor: Tell me more about your main character. Where can you use the most help? Tell me why that scene is important?

Did I ask those kinds of questions because that is the conferencing style I've evolved over the years? Or was I unable to engage in critical dialog because I wasn't smart enough, knowledgeable enough, and perceptive enough to say something substantive about students' writing?

On the final evaluation a handful of students nailed me in ways that seemed far from my personality. Given the vindictiveness of some of the class members, these comments didn't hurt much:

> "The teacher's attitude varied—I wondered if this man is sick of teaching."

> "It was difficult to write creative material knowing feedback would not be tactful."

> "I was unimpressed with the instructor. Policy seemed more important than people." (This one made me squirm as I thought of my dictatorial syllabus loaded with so many deadlines, requirements, and procedural instructions.)

Other student's comments were right on the money, and this sent me into depression and guilt. My self-esteem plummeted.

> "Class discussion wasn't very productive during workshops of individual fiction pieces. I felt time would have been better spent if workshops had been more structured."

I wasn't good at running large class discussions of students' writing, despite one student's comment that class discussions were good and that I was a "very open instructor." I looked at large group discussions as something I had to control, something that I was responsible for making successful. The thought of just letting discussions evolve panicked me. Surprise frightened me. The unknown was ominous. I was better at setting up and training peer response groups and conferring individually with students. In fact, many students commented that the peer groups were the best part of the class (a time, I noted, when I wasn't present). Large group discussion was not my forte. It showed. One student suggested that I "might pass out some peer response rules and cite one when people get out of line."

As the weeks passed, class continued to go badly. No one knew that better than me. Paranoia befriended me. When I left the building late one night, I saw three graduate students lounging against a car in the parking lot. I turned my head and picked up my pace. They weren't fooling anybody. I knew the subject of their talk. They were making plans to complain about my course to the department head. Or maybe to the director of graduate studies. No, I'll bet it was the dean they were going to see.

One morning, a good friend of mine in the department, a senior faculty member and chair of my tenure and promotion committee, appeared in my office doorway. He wore an anguished, apologetic expression. He was sorry, he said, for what I was going through and he'd like to take me to lunch. I gulped and agreed. The rest of the morning I fretted about how much he knew. I was guilty of lousy teaching amid everyone else's great teaching. And now my best friend was going to have a difficult talk with me about the rumors he'd heard. I didn't want to be helped to teach better. I just didn't want to be caught by my peers in such incompetence. How would such horrible teaching affect my status in the department? What would my tenure and promotion committee say?

At lunch my friend brought up another matter, a personal one that had nothing to do with school. He knew nothing about the debacle I conducted each Monday night. I let him know that I appreciated his sympathy. Then I swallowed pasta salad and kept my mouth shut about the monstrous class I'd created.

On another day I had lunch with a friend from secondary education. He taught English teaching methods. I told him of the anxiety I was feeling because of one class. I told him some of the facts, but not too many. He let me blather, then unloaded to me how badly his present English methods class was going, the students in open revolt because of the massive workload.

I felt relief. I'm ashamed to add that the relief didn't come because I had been able to unburden myself. The reason for my relief wasn't cathartic. It was ignominious. Another teacher in the world—a good teacher whom I respected—was having a difficult time teaching a class. Ha! Ha! See? Not only I was capable of such educational malfeasance! Others were wretched and incompetent, too.

But the relief didn't last. My friend's class was going badly because he was demanding. My class was spinning out of control because of me, because I lacked credibility. One student wrote that "Professor Romano is caring and understanding toward his students." Right, I thought bitterly. What I wanted to be was astute, incisive, and cogent. Another student wrote that the weekly one-on-one conference was great "because I had to face the teacher and I always wanted it to be with something great." So Romano could then ask his insipid questions, he might have added.

Two evaluations exhibited what seemed to me the utmost disdain for the class and for me. The grid on the evaluation form was blackened with responses of Disagree and Strongly Disagree and then for this, a writing class, the students had made no comments on the remaining two pages. How lowly, how base, how mean and snivelling to be disdained, dismissed, and scorned.

In a most humane and helpful way two students addressed the problem that was at the core of the disastrous class and that I didn't want to face and didn't want anyone to know about. "I'd like to see the pushy 'bitchy' trio reined in a bit more," wrote one of them. "They're so rude they intimidate the more sensitive." The other wrote that the teacher "needs more experience with students at this level, needs to be more assertive and take a stand."

My heartbeat sped up. Students knew what I knew. I lacked courage. Pedagogical courage. When the quality of talk degenerated in workshops, when cliques formed amid the mix of graduates and undergraduates, when my individual conferencing style didn't work—instead of letting go and enlisting the students' aid in solving the problem of the deteriorating class, fear ruled me—fear of losing control, fear of recriminations for incompetence, fear of being revealed a fraud. But I had already lost control. I had already revealed incompetence. I was already playing the fraud.

Instead of acknowledging my fears and failings and confronting them with courage, I became defensive. I closed communication and sought to turn the class around by exerting autocratic control (which is like a fascist political leader invoking martial law to preserve his corrupt government). I gave more direct lectures, conducted more in-class lessons that kept students busy, required more written assignments. And the stringent measures didn't work. The ship sank . . . with me singing stridently on the bridge at the top of my lungs. My unwillingness to admit and confront demon fear did me in.

Even if I had mustered the necessary courage, that advanced fiction writing class would have been difficult to teach, given my idiosyncrasies, the personalities of some of the students, the fact that I wasn't an advanced fiction writer myself and that it was my first year of university teaching. But no matter. Because I capitulated to fear, I didn't have a chance of improving the class.

One student—God bless her—wrote on her evaluation, "I'd absolutely take this teacher again. He lets me feel like I'm teaching myself."

Believe me, I thought, you were. You were.

References

Burroway, Janet. 1992. *Writing Fiction: A Guide to Narrative Craft*. New York: HarperCollins.

Murray, Don. 1990. *Shoptalk*. Portsmouth, NH: Heinemann.

Day One Dud

JANE A. KEARNS

L
ike a nervous race horse charging from the just-opened gate, I always
want to get my classes to start immediately, day one, minute one.
Students are anxious, worried about who their teachers will be, and
ready to get going. I try to accommodate them by wasting no time on
day one.

Right away I get them brainstorming topics, listing possible pieces of
writing, topics, and themes, creating time lines of events and people in their
lives, thinking of people they know who could be subjects of future pieces.

And I think students want homework on that first day, not mounds and
mountains, just something to tell Mom and Dad, something to complain
about, and something to do after a long summer of *not much*.

Another part of my great plan in the steeplechase derby of teaching
concerns repeating activities or assignments. I don't. I do not want to do the
same thing in each class. Students talk; their grapevine is better than any
small town's. Once they realize that you repeat the work in every class, the
word spreads and they are ready for whatever you present.

I want fresh thinking, even surprises to strain their brains. These come,
I believe, from exclusive approaches, so for the early days of the year I always
present different activities and different assignments to each class. If students
really checked, they would see that the activities, though different, are similar
in goals or directions. This great plan, however, sometimes crumbles into
flying dust kicked in my face—as it did this time.

That year, based on recent classes of the same type of students (freshmen
from a variety of eighth grades: a large inner-city junior high, two small
parochial schools, and four small country elementary schools), I intended to
build my writing unit with an early emphasis on details.

My purpose was to get an early look at some writing to see if my
judgment about students not understanding the need and power of details

31

was true with these groups and whether I indeed did have to stress details as part of the development of longer pieces.

For each of five classes I created a separate but similar homework assignment for that first day of school, one that involved as much activity as it did writing—observations topped off with a listing of details:

- If you have a pet dog or cat, watch the pet for a half hour around suppertime and record the pet's actions. List words that describe it. (You can use a neighbor's pet or you can observe a brother or sister, if you prefer.)

- Determine where your neighborhood ends. What makes it your neighborhood and what makes it different/similar from others? List words that describe it. (You can use a backyard or someone else's backyard, if you prefer.)

- Look around your home. Find something that you hadn't noticed before. Examine it and try to find out how long it has been in your home and who put it there. List words that describe it. (You can use a garage, a workplace, or a car, if you prefer.)

- Go to the tree nearest your front door. Sit near it, under it. How is it similar to other trees? How is it so very different? List words to describe it. (You can pick a nearby tree or plant or flower or bush, if you prefer.)

I had used many of these before, often as choices, and like all writing activity prompts, some work with some students, none work with all students. But I wasn't looking for total success. I was trying to nudge them toward knowing they have things around them that may be possible writing topics and toward understanding that they do know about certain things familiar to them. These can be starting points for writing.

The assignment for the fifth class was, I thought, like the others. Though I had never used it before, it fit with the core activity I was hoping for, calling for a few minutes of observation, then a list of some words, thoughts, ideas that might later be developed into a longer piece or become part of another topic:

- Sit outside on your back steps or porch just as dusk falls and there is that evening darkness. Listen. What sounds do you hear? After ten minutes or so, go inside and record all the sounds you heard.

Like all student assignments, I did each one so I could be part of the conversation on day two, not an outsider pretending to be a writer and an observer. It worked as I figured. Some students had funny stories: "My brother almost beat me up for staring at him." "My dog paid no attention to anyone except my mother until she fed him, then he went to my dad." "I remember the old fort my friends and I built in that tree." "I can't believe I didn't notice the new carpet in the front room—my mother said it was put in last year! They don't tell me anything."

In my first four classes, there was a mixture of results, but all students heard about unique observations and how important it is to be observant—we were off on our year's writing.

But . . . in the fifth class, I knew something was wrong. I could hear it in their silence. All the other classes complained and laughed and couldn't wait to tell their stories. Not here. And I knew myself that the assignment didn't work for me. All I had heard was the boring whirring of truck tires.

As the bell rang and I stood in front of the silent group, I took a chance and asked, "Did anyone have the same problem with last night's homework as I did? Nothing of interest to hear?"

You could see their relief, and their stories, different ones, tumbled out: "All I heard were trucks and cars on the highway." "Me too. Nothing but traffic." "I couldn't hear over the sound of street noise. Cars." "Me too." "Yeah." "I don't have a back porch." "It was awful."

I laughed and nodded, and we agreed that was one bad assignment. I apologized. This was the first time I ever used that assignment, I told them, "and I think I'll rip it up and toss it away."

"Yeah, that's good. I thought I was the only one."

"Phew. I feel better."

"Throw it in the trash can."

"Let's junk that one."

"Don't ever assign that again."

I had learned my lesson, try assignments first. In the silence, in between this second outburst and catching my breath to begin day one again, on day two, a voice whispered, "I liked it." I couldn't see the speaker but when I moved up the aisle where the whisper came from I saw him. A small-framed, blond-headed boy who looked about ten years old. He sat low in his seat and over to the side so the student in front hid his whole body.

"Billy. What did you say?"

"I heard a lot."

"Tell us about it." The whole class turned to listen.

"I live in Deerfield."

"No," said another student, "you live *way, way, way* out in Deerfield."

Again, together, we laughed and enjoyed this give-and-take; the city students and I didn't know about this geography, so we were really intrigued now.

"Well, anyway, I sat out on my back porch steps and listened, just like you said. Quiet at first, then I began to hear horses clomping around the barn exercise area; some birds, I think they were northern mockingbirds; my grandfather in the barn patting down the cows. Then in between these regular sounds, I heard something that surprised me. I heard the brook down behind the fenced-in area. The brook sounded cool and busy and . . . gurgly and . . . I liked that."

"Wow that sounds great."

"I always wanted to live on a farm."

"I think you did a great job."

"He did the best assignment."

"We can count his grade for the whole class."

We all wanted to know more, so we started asking questions. (This interchange was an important beginning to the type of sharing I wanted to develop.)

"How did you know what kind of birds?"

"How many animals do you have?"

"Where in Deerfield do you live?"

One boy who also came from Deerfield answered this last question: "He lives so far away, the school bus doesn't even go that far."

"I live so far out," Billy added, "I have to get up at five to get to the place where I get the bus." Others who knew him joined in. "He lives so far out his home is really in Canada." "He lives so far away that he gets his wakeup call before he goes to bed." These metaphoric exaggerations became a touchstone that reverberated all year.

"I'll tell you where I live. You know where the fairground road is?" Billy asked. Most students did, because they all attended that town's annual farm fair. "Take a left at the top of the hill, go all the way down there, then take Old Parsons Road until the end and go right along the dirt road for about six miles. Our place is the only one there."

While the assignment bombed with everyone else, for Billy it was a landmark. Not only did he give us a lesson in country living and sounds of the farm, but he brought the class together. Unlike other classes where the tuition students often felt left out, in this class, because of Billy's story and the class's involvement, they were welcomed and become friends.

All the diversity in the class, students from different backgrounds and schools and experiences, from inner-city tenements and three-acre town lots and rural family farms, came together as a community. Outside they might be in different cliques but for these forty-three minutes the students worked together. Though he remained quiet and shy, Billy had a special place in this class, and the harmony lasted all year. His living on a farm wasn't a source of individual embarrassment but a seed for class pride.

Though I've never used this assignment since, I'll always appreciate the soft quiet voice, "I liked it." The assignment bombed except for one bright shining moment when a farm boy took us all to his back porch.

Slapping Gary

MARNI GILLARD

Gary sat in the third seat of the row against the inside wall of my eighth-grade classroom, as far from window distractions and the attentions of the other "bad" boys in class as I could get him. I could tell from things he said and from the little work he had turned in that Gary was smart, but as the school year progressed he was doing less and less. "Surly" would describe him. So far he had responded to my efforts to get him to like English (or at least to do his work) with growl-like sounds and shoulder jerks, silent stares and sneers. I had not seen Gary be cruel but I had observed a bully quality in him during hallway interactions with weaker students. I also knew he had been reported, with a group of other male eighth graders, for pulling the pants off a younger boy during a bus ride home from a sports event. I had seated Gary near girls I hoped wouldn't talk with him and the kind of boys who wouldn't either, but there weren't enough "good" kids to separate all the troubled boys in my class. Even the experienced teachers talked about that year's eighth-grade class. It was the fall of 1974, my second year of teaching.

That second year was scary from the second day on. (My pep talk to students about what a great year it was going to be held their attention the first day.) Basically, I faced another first year of teaching, because I had a new principal who, it turns out, didn't have much faith in me. When I began to have trouble almost immediately, I felt so alone. I slowly began to lose faith in myself as a teacher. Although I'd never done it my first year, I sent troublesome, uncooperative students to the principal's office because they were such a distraction to the other students and they interfered with my ability to teach with enthusiasm, something I intuitively sensed was my strong suit. After my second request for disciplinary support, I got this lecture from the principal: "Kids aren't supposed to *like* school. Your job is to keep control. It's as simple as that. They will respect you for making them work and not taking any of their nonsense. Aim for their respect, not their friendship. I've given two of your students a good talking to, but the office is not here to baby-sit the kids you can't handle. Quit trying to be nice. If you can't get and keep control of a class, you can't stay in teaching." My department coordinator, a gentle man who was my one connection to the memory of my sweet first year of teaching, looked at me with sadness when I complained to him. He'd taught my tough boys the year before in his seventh grade and was happy to be rid of them. He offered to talk to one of the ringleaders but that only made things worse. I recall, vaguely, that he gave me some advice, but whatever it was, it didn't help.

I don't remember now exactly why I chose Gary to slap. I think I had reached some limit of powerlessness and had to take a stand. I remember passing his desk, glancing down to see if he was once again refusing to attempt whatever task I'd assigned. I had accepted the role of security guard because several children in that class simply didn't do "their" work. Of course I know now that it was more *my* work, not work they had any stake in, but it would be years before the concept of student-generated curriculum would enter my consciousness.

During neither my eight-week student-teaching experience at an urban high school nor my first year of employment had students openly defied my attempts to get them to work. A few might have resisted, but I'd cajoled them or gotten a little stern, and they had "buckled down," as my grandfather used to say. Gary wasn't doing his work that day, and he had refused to work on so many others. The smirk on his face that I read to proclaim, You can't make me, probably prompted my action.

Some people wouldn't call it a "slap." Adults easily excuse the "small" ways we invade children's personal spaces and their bodies. I tapped Gary's left cheek with the back of my hand. It was a small private gesture, and I believe I whispered something to the effect of, Hey, kid, *I'm* the one in control here, not you. Get to *work*.

My slapping Gary's cheek touched off something in him. He stood up and punched me in the face with most, if not all, of his strength. I don't know why he didn't break my nose or knock any teeth out. My brother, at age fourteen, relieved me of a few last baby teeth with not nearly as strong a punch the year I threw his new ski sweater in the toilet. I was jealous that I couldn't go on an all-male ski trip with my brothers, their friends, and my father. When Gary hit me, my face felt numb but it didn't hurt. I didn't cry. On the contrary, I felt a surge of inner control that I hadn't felt since the first day of school. I didn't stop to think, at that moment, about the inexcusable thing I'd done. I only knew that Gary's response had given me power, not stripped me of it. Gary, I believe, also felt the shift. Stunned by the fact that he had just hit a young female teacher publicly, he slumped into his chair and put his head down and cried. I leaned over and firmly but gently said, "I think you need to sit in the hall. I want to talk to the class. I'll be out in a minute." He nodded. As he walked toward the door, very little in his movements still labeled him "surly adolescent"; his face and posture read more like "small hurt boy."

I have reflected for many years on what happened next. I spoke to the class in a quiet, calm adult voice. "Gary has done something that he is going to be very ashamed of." The girls and many boys looked astonished that I appeared to be unscathed by this and concerned about Gary and perhaps them rather than myself. "He needs to calm down and I'm certain he will. I am going to go out in the hall so we can talk about what just happened. I want you to work quietly and not talk about this. Can you do that?" They nodded passively. I returned the nod with a look that told them I believed in them and would protect them. When I think about this moment, I see both positive and negative sides to it. I did care about their welfare and realize this could be an image they would carry all their lives. Intuitively I knew I had to help them take away some positive meaning from it. Yet I also begin to understand how abusers of children get away with what they do for so long. Children want adults to take control and to assure them they are safe, even when they are not.

In the hall Gary was quiet. His punch had unleashed his fury but also drained him. I could now be generous. "Do you think you and I can sort this out, or do you need to go sit in the principal's office and have him deal with it?" I took a risk in offering Gary this option, because I did not want Gary in the principal's office any more than he wanted to be there. Gary just shook his head. I began to feel real affection for him for the first time that year. I did not want to hurt him anymore. I only wanted the joy of teaching back. I think my desperate need to have my classroom back was stronger than Gary's need for power over me.

I did what so many abusers do: I required his silence. In a quiet but threatening voice I said, "Okay, I will not tell the principal about this. We can put it behind us. But it's time you did your work. You are a smart boy who is wasting his life." I paused to let him hear, if he could, that I genuinely cared about him and that I recognized his abilities. "Truce?" I asked. He nodded. I told him to remain in the hall for the last few moments of class and then to come back in for his books when the bell rang. I returned to class to clean up the emotional mess Gary and I had left behind. I had to reassert that I, not Gary, had won the victory. I knew this could be a pivotal moment in not only the year but my career. The scared looks on so many of the kids' faces told me they needed comforting, but my survival was what I cared most about at the moment.

I walked back into the room and had everyone's attention immediately. "This incident is over. As far as Gary and I are concerned it is mended. He has apologized and I have accepted. I do not want this incident to go beyond these walls. Is that clear?" I didn't know whether to believe the students' nods but I hoped the incident was closed. I now see my asking for their silence as one more part of the pattern of abuse. Luckily, one girl told or I might not have learned all I have from this experience.

Two days later the union building representative, Bill, suddenly joined me as I walked down the crowded hallway toward the cafeteria. "Hey, how's it going?" he asked in a friendly way. He had never spoken to me personally before. He taught eighth-grade math on a different hall from mine. His bumping into me was no accident. He was a small, wiry man, not much taller than I, with a reputation for being a clown. At faculty meetings he joked irreverently about serious and difficult topics the way the doctors in M*A*S*H quipped about the bloody innards of bodies maimed in wartime. His friendliness was an attempt to relax me, but I tensed up, wondering what his appearance at my side implied. "I'm okay," I said.

He looked at me for a moment longer, perhaps choosing his words with care. "You know, we have this thing called a union." Those words elicited the smile he had hoped for so he forged ahead. "In a union people stick together. We take care of each other." He paused to see if I was making sense of his words. I knew he was trying to say that I wasn't in the wrong, but I realized his words meant that I'd been found out. He went on. "We don't let the children hit us. We support each other when things get tough. I can get that kid out of your class."

I felt humiliated. I felt as if the entire world knew that I couldn't teach and never would be a good teacher. I wasn't thinking of Gary or of any of the children in that moment. I was ashamed that I had been caught striking a child, an unforgivable act that I had tried to "get away with."

I asked, "How did you know?" Again, he smiled in a clownish way and tried to lighten the situation. "Oh, Karen lives next door. Her parents told me." Karen was one of those hardworking girls I had tried to use as insulation around Gary. She knew instinctively that this was no secret to keep.

"What do you want to do about this?" Bill asked. "Do you want some help? Do you want the principal brought in? You're in charge."

"No," I said instantly. "I've handled it. I want to see if I can establish a new relationship with both Gary and the class. In the two days since it happened things have been better. I don't want the principal to know. He already thinks I can't handle things."

"Okay," he said, and his smile was genuine, no longer teasing. "I just want you to know we are here for you. You don't have to do it all alone."

Here, in a nutshell, is what I took away from this experience. Gary and his friends, bullies all, had been stripped of their wholesome power somewhere along the way. When learning in my class didn't come easy for them despite my enthusiastic first-day promises, they had tried to seize power by refusing to work, by hiding behind the shield of their hurts. They had learned to claim power from those weaker than themselves, as they had from the young boy on the bus. Gary understood that their resistance was weakening me. I slapped him from a place of weakness, but his punch in the nose awakened what was truly strong in me. I wanted to be a teacher, not one who wields control over children or takes it from them, but one who stands firmly in the power of love and teaches others how to feel enthusiasm for learning. Gary's punch told me, as Bill did explicitly two days later, "You're in charge."

It would take me a few years to learn that helping "surly" students find themselves in literature and their voices through writing and storytelling was a more effective teaching strategy than barricading them with "good" students. Talking with friends and looking at life outside the window might just offer the inspiration that would help resistant students connect to the work in "my" English class. Gary became one of my many teachers in what is still an ongoing learning journey.

Teaching the Story You Have Not Read

KIM R. STAFFORD

When I stepped into the seminar room, I was afraid. The distance between my well-schooled mind and my sweaty feet was interrupted by a void at belt level. I was totally unprepared for class. This was an upper-division Chaucer class at a university where I hoped one day to teach full time: the beginning of my brilliant career. Fresh from graduate school, I had grand plans. I was on my flight to glory, and I was about to crash.

Several weeks before, as a coda to my lecture on varieties of Chaucerian narrative, I had told the class a story I'd heard from Jim Heynen, who had confessed to me what happened when he read the wrong story for his course in modern fiction. In a busy week, he had read a great Flannery O'Connor story beginning on page 227. The students, with their revised edition, had read a different O'Connor story. As he approached the room, he could hear them talking about their story. "Very strange," one said, as she listed some of the more outrageous episodes. Jim realized he had *never* read that story. Taking inward counsel, as he paused in the doorway, he saw two options: he could confess his error and muddle through somehow; or he could pretend he had read the correct story and see what happened. The second seemed the far more interesting option.

My students had enjoyed my report of Jim's next steps. (Any time I strayed from the exact lesson at hand, they seemed to think we were on vacation.) Jim had started class by asking for a volunteer to make a list on the board of the characters in the story. "Who's in this story, anyway?" An alert student, realizing this was the easy task of the hour, went to the board to list the names and turned around with a grin when he finished. "Hey," one student said, "what about that old man?" The volunteer was on the spot. "He wasn't really a character in the story," he said, "because he didn't have a name." "Hey," said another student, "God doesn't have a name in the whole Talmud." Lively discussion followed. Jim found himself giving a short lecture, in the form of a series of questions and examples from other stories, of the deep importance of very "minor" characters in short narratives. "Remember the ticket seller in *Death in Venice?* We don't know his name, but try to imagine the story without him." In his ignorance, Jim was free to turn from the assigned story to the immediate question raised by the class and to bring to that question the full range of his reading and thinking. When he paused from his impromptu lecture, they were ten minutes into the hour.

The volunteer, still stunned at the board, added "old man" to the character list and sat down. Jim asked the class, "Is this useful, simply to have a list of characters in front of us, as we prepare to discuss the story?" Yes, the class thought it was useful. "Well," said Professor Heynen, "I wonder, in that case, if someone might make us a list of the scenes in this story. Let's have two volunteers this time, helping each other." Two students went together to the board, wrote, muttered, conferred. They did a good job, but again, when they turned around, there was a question from the class. "What about that scene in the doorway, when the lady is about to leave?" "That wasn't a scene," said one student, "that was a transition." "Ah," said Jim, "what's the difference?" Lively discussion again. This time, it was a student who gave the short lecture on something she had been noticing in this story and others, how a transition was like a "bridge" in a song, raising the whole piece to a new pitch or key. The transition itself could be very short and still have a big effect, like the short-story genre itself. "We're talking essence here!" There was a moment of silence, as this sank in. Then everyone wanted to talk about what this meant. Did this kind of transition, this climbing to a new level, happen in every story? Did it happen in novels? Did it happen in a political campaign, a war, a relationship? If it didn't happen, did the whole thing fall apart, like Vietnam? Like Humphrey's campaign? Or McGovern's? Did it happen in one's own life? How could you recognize it, encourage it? Is that what Flannery O'Connor was getting at, with that one little turn in her story filled with terrors? Maybe you could make slight adjustments in life that turned sorrow to safety. Wasn't she sick all the time, in her own life? And yet she wrote stories. What if you started to notice things in your own life like that moment in the doorway, when everything started to change?

There was much to say, and everyone chimed in, except Jim. He watched with mounting satisfaction. Another fifteen minutes down, and class was going *very* well. And when things got settled, when the class remembered their instructor was present, Jim was ready with the key question. Gesturing toward the two lists on the board, like an orchestra conductor about to launch the grand march, he asked the group to decide: "In which scene do you feel these characters enter into the essential conflict that makes the story what it is?" What followed, Jim told me with some chagrin, was the best class he had ever taught.

That was a good story, but this was now. Taking a deep breath, I stepped into the classroom and immediately confessed my crime. "Remember that story I told you about my friend teaching the story he had never read?" They nodded solemnly. "Yes, well, in the past eight hours I had to choose whether to mark your papers from two weeks ago or reread books four and five of *Troilus and Criseyde*. That's just how the past week went. Sorry. I knew you'd kill me if I didn't give your papers back, so I read your work instead of reading Chaucer. There is some great stuff in here." I hefted the stack of papers before them. "But it's been years since I read those last two books of *Troilus,* so you are going to have to teach class tonight instead of me."

Mingled groans and whoops. I passed back their papers. They studied my comments for a few moments, then put the papers away and looked at me. Five minutes had passed in a three-hour class. It was a warm evening in spring, and we had the windows open. "Don't look at me," I said, "this is *your* night." The silence hung heavy. A car passed on the street outside. Everyone realized if a student so much as glanced at the textbook or at another student, the tide would turn, and they would have to take me up on my offer. We were a tableau: a wax museum of collegiate education. They looked at me. I looked at them. As Chaucer says, "Pity renneth soone in gentil herte." I felt for them. They had paid a huge sum to be instructed, and I was letting them down. I was ignorant, but I was supposed to be in charge. We had let the silence reign for long enough, and I surrendered with a question. "Doesn't Criseyde leave Troilus in book four? I do seem to remember that."

"Yeah, man, that part's tough."

"I wonder," I said, "if any of you ever had to say good-bye to a lover." These were juniors and seniors: a ripple of groans and sighs. "How about," I said, "if you each write a letter of farewell to a lover, and then you can begin class with a discussion of what you learned by writing this?" Relieved to be so directed, even toward such a quirky task, they bent to paper. I looked around the room. Scowls replaced their calm. My students turned visibly into anguished lovers. They scratched with fury. I remembered early sorrows, and I joined them in writing my own farewell. It was summer, and the story of my life was crumbling. If only she could understand. . . .

In ten minutes I looked up from my own sad story to be greeted with a spectacle that chilled my bones: twenty-seven papers were being handed toward me! I felt like the mouth of a river that could not contain the flood. No, I thought. Please no. I just returned those research papers. Mercy!

My prayers were answered in the voice of an inspired student. "Wait!" he said, "instead of passing these letters in to *him,* why doesn't everyone pass them to *me*. I'll read them aloud anonymously, and we can vote on whether we think they were written by a woman or a man."

By the alchemy of his genius, the tide of paper changed direction, and I sent my own note hustling along with the others, toward my redeemer. He read them one by one, inflecting several with a credible Chaucerian tone— hopeless Arcite, the lusty Wife, "handy" Nicholas, grim Griselde, the shrewd young May, even a Parson's sermon. What letters! We had our own miniature collection of salty tales from the pilgrimage of modern life. As our Mr. Lonelyhearts read aloud, our vote was intuitive, scrabbling for clues from the literary tenor of cryptic romance. Our vote was often accurate, for we guessed what we did not know. Men, it seems, write mushy, lingering farewells: I will never forget the time we first met. . . . Women, by contrast, write stern endings: I should have seen a long time ago that you didn't care about who I was at all. . . . I didn't have to say it, for a student said it first: "Hey, it looks like courtly love lives on in men, but not in women—six hundred years after Chaucer died! All that love stuff! The guys are as bad as Troilus!" She was right. Lively discussion. Class going well.

"Okay," I said when things died down, "with that for a start, how about if we now make a list of some of the ways to teach literature, as you have observed this activity yourselves from many years of watching teachers do it well or ill?" They looked at each other with a strange eagerness, and I looked at them. The veil of my professorial urgency fell like scales from my eyes, and I saw their wisdom. I think they saw it, too. A student went to the board, the ready secretary for us all.

"You can check out one story against another," said one, "and like, maybe learn something there." Our secretary wrote, "Compare two stories."

"Yeah, or you can just read a part you love and ask people what they hear. Sometimes you just love the sound of it." Our secretary wrote: "Love the poetry."

"Recite some rock lyrics, man, and compare."

"You can ask kind of a question—like about Chaucer's thing about women—and get the *class* to find places in the poem where it happens."

"Yeah, get the class to do it. That's the whole idea."

"Or you can ask people what they thought about when they were reading. Just, like, start calling on people."

"You can scope out an idea from some other scene—like music—and jive it to the story."

"Hey, I know! You can list the characters, and then the scenes, and then make a big question out of it."

For the next two hours, I watched some of the finest teaching I have ever seen. That tenured spot went to someone with better preparation than mine, and now I travel to see how people learn.

Searching for John/Herb/Frank

PATRICK SHANNON

graduated in the spring of 1973 with one B.A. in eighteenth- and nine-teenth-century intellectual history and another in economic theory and began teaching kindergarten the following fall in an inner-city school. It was a federal project that paid $3,000 for the school year, remitted tuition for an M.A.T. degree (to be completed during that first year), and presented me with my own class of thirty-five five-year-olds. I had not completed a meth-ods class before the first day; I had no practice teaching; and I had not even visited an elementary school in ten years. I guess I'd be called an "emergency certificate" in today's parlance. Then, I was just another refugee from one of Nixon's recessions, and I liked to go to school.

I had learned from four years of college that one way to address my fears—and I was terrified of those kindergartners after the first day—was to go to the library. *Kindergarten Cop* had not yet been shot. On the recom-mendation of Mrs. Clark, a reference librarian at the city library, I borrowed and read three books my first weekend off—John Holt's *How Children Fail* (1964), Herb Kohl's *36 Children* (1967), and Frank Smith's *Understanding Read-ing* (1971). She also recommended Sylvia Ashton Warner's *Teacher* (1964), but it was out. By the second week, I had created an image of a good teacher for myself, and I have been trying to realize that image for over twenty years now—with some success.

I can laugh now about some of the sore spots of my first year of teaching. For example, I tried to help a silent boy by feeding him so many things to say during sharing that he panicked, asked to go to the bathroom, but instead left school and walked to his grandmother's. I had an entire kindergarten class all "doing the A's" at the same time when most of them could already read and write stories. I tried to use clay for mathematics during a tenure observation and all the kids would do was make and talk about replicas of penises. Those and many other attempts to be John/Herb/Frank made me cry, and I'll admit, made me drink too much. Failures weren't just a daily occur-

44

rence; they happened every hour. But at the time, I believed that I could actually become the vision in my head—to be like John/Herb/Frank—if I worked hard enough.

I developed as a teacher during the year because I had an image of what I wanted to do, because I could talk about it with some detail among friends, and because I'm pretty stubborn about not giving up (although I still can't hit a curve ball). Beginning in October of that first year, we studied a pond for science in a park down the street from our school. We took samples of water and studied them under a microscope. We captured bugs and slimy things and studied them while we kept them alive in jars. We identified plants and animals by looking in books and asking people who actually knew something about this stuff. We measured the water temperature and depth. All in order to see what the seasons did to the pond, the wildlife, and the community around it. However, we also fell in the pond repeatedly, got muddy up to our knees repeatedly, forgot to bring paper to record our data repeatedly, told our parents we did nothing today in school repeatedly, stood mute before an audience at the school science fair only once, were told that we made a duck desert her eggs because we were too noisy and unthoughtful, complained about the "too long" walk repeatedly, cried because the rain or snow prevented us from taking the walk often, and had to go to the bathroom as soon as we arrived at the pond every single visit. Failure or success?

I've written about some of my failures as a teacher educator—my inability to engage administrators in critical action research in their schools, my trouble helping teachers believe that change in literacy programs is possible, my blindness to our son's social construction of literacy during the first few weeks of his kindergarten experience, and my failure to convince teachers in my graduate classes that what I do could be called "teaching" (this one still hurts).

I fail to some extent during every class. That is, I do not offer invitations that everyone accepts; I miss opportunities to respond to students' work in ways that help them look at it again in new ways; I lose the image of John/Herb/Frank and tell 'em what I know. These failures are compounded by the fact that I attempt to create doubt among students where there is certainty—to reconsider how literacy is defined, who is literate and who is not, what is read and written, and how literacy is acquired and taught. This is hard work for students and for me, and often we fail to communicate. To push past our commonsense answers to these questions, we ask questions to which we don't know the answers, look for answers in places we don't feel comfortable going, and begin to recognize that ambiguity is part of life, literacy, and learning.

I do not consider myself a failure though, because I keep searching for the John/Herb/Frank inside me and because I work to create institutions that will let me keep searching. And I say, Failures of the world unite, we have nothing to lose. . . .

References

Holt, John. 1964. *How Children Fail.* New York: Dutton.

Kohl, Herb. 1967. *36 Children.* New York: Signet.

Smith, Frank. 1971. *Understanding Reading.* New York: Holt, Rinehart & Winston.

Warner, Sylvia Ashton. 1964. *Teacher.* New York: Bantam.

Rewriting Teaching

DONALD M. MURRAY

Six weeks into the first course in a journalism curriculum the University of New Hampshire hired me to design, I startled my students by saying, "If you will forget how I have screwed up, I will forget how you have screwed up."

Then I marched them into a new classroom and began the first semester of academic year 1963–64 over again.

Dave Cohen, now an editor on *The Boston Globe,* who was in that class, has told me that he planned to drop the course until I made my announcement. He didn't stay with hope the course would actually improve but with wonder. Later he told me he'd had many courses in which the instructor had screwed up but none where the instructor admitted it.

I did not make this move in wisdom but in terror. I had prepared all summer. I had a real wooden lectern. I had detailed lecture notes. I knew my subject. I had lived News Writing 101. I even met with my students in conferences and told them what was wrong with their stories face to face.

There was one problem. The stories were not improving. My students were not learning.

Remember, I was inexperienced, a journalist who was hired to teach at the age of thirty-nine. In a few years I would become a member of the academic club, and I would know that if the students were not learning it was their fault, not mine.

But I had come from a world where it wasn't the readers' fault if they didn't understand what I was saying. It was my fault. If my students weren't learning it was *not* their fault. It was mine. I would start over.

That seemed logical to me. I felt little surprise they weren't learning. I was a beginning teacher and I had to learn the teaching craft as I had learned the writer's craft. I would start a new draft.

I had been a full-time free-lance writer for nine years. Beside my desk I had a fifty-five-gallon cardboard and metal-rimmed drum. I agreed with Isaac

Bashevis Singer, who said, "I am my own first reader, and pleasing me is a hard job. If a story doesn't satisfy me, I have a good friend under my desk: the wastepaper basket."

I felt no shame in failure but accepted it as essential. How else did one learn except by failing? I read each magazine article thirty times before the first submission and many more times after it was criticized by an editor. Each failed draft was instructive and so was each class and each conference.

From the lectern, I gave my students precise, clearly enunciated instructions on how to write a specific news story—speech, fire, court—in a parade-ground voice. Then I commanded them to go do it. They worked hard but did not follow my instructions. The stories failed.

In talking with them—and listening—I discovered they didn't understand my instructions. They had to attempt the reporting and writing task and fail. Then, in their individual failures, they could discover the reasons the stories didn't work. Then they could decide what would make the stories work. They came up with my instructions but now the instructions were theirs. I revised my teaching and started to offer instruction after failure, when my students were ready to learn.

In conferences, I struggled to figure out the reasons my students worked hard to produce such tangled, constipated prose. They listened politely to my explanations—and repeated the prose.

Then I got drafts that were so bad I couldn't conceive of why they were written that way. In desperation, I started asking students why and found they knew the answers. They knew what they were doing wrong. The worst papers were born of not ignorance and laziness but careful, cautious, logic—they wrote in generalities, for example, because they had a general audience—that didn't work.

If I listened to their own reasons they wrote the way they did, I was instructed. And if I asked them to solve the problems they had just described, they could. The less I taught, the more I gave them room to attempt to learn, to fail, and to revise their learning, the better writers they became. I was not an instructor but a listener, an encourager, a resource, a reader, a monitor to their own learning.

I began to catch on. I was learning to teach as I learned to write—by revision. I gave the required final exam—a strange and inappropriate inheritance in a writing course—to incoming students. They did better than the students who had received 220 hours of my lectures over two semesters. I started rewriting the course—and my teaching methods.

For years I would decide what worked best in each course the semester before and cut it out of the course. That way I learned what was really working for the students, not for me. My colleagues found this bizarre, but I was trying to turn a success into a failure to see if could learn something from it.

And I did. I thought I had taught a specific technique, a way of cutting copy for brevity, but the next semester I taught a different—and sometimes a contradictory—technique, and my new students learned as well as my previous ones. I interviewed them and discovered I hadn't been teaching techniques as much as attitudes. My students discovered the delight of brevity and then figured out how to achieve it in their own way.

And as I took the successes out of my course, I discovered that listening was better than lecturing, that my students' revising their papers was better than my revising them, that their attempts to design a solution to their writing problems were better than my exercises and assignments, that their evaluation of what they needed to learn and how they might learn it was more perceptive than mine. I created an environment in which they learned—and I learned from their learning.

And they taught me writing as well as teaching.

Often I had my students write a new, individual syllabus halfway through the course in which they decided on their key problems and decided how they would solve them. Their syllabi were more demanding than syllabi I would ever dare impose.

I continued to rewrite my drafts and learn to write; I continued to rewrite my courses and learn to teach. Neither craft can ever be learned. Like doctors, we have a practice.

And practicing my dual crafts keeps me interested in writing and teaching. I was learning with my students.

The last semester I taught I had an unexpected visitor from Texas who wanted to observe me teaching my Freshman English class. She was disappointed. No lectures. Mostly just listening.

She went through the syllabus, which had already been rewritten, asking me how this worked, how that worked, how successful this had been, how I was sure. . . . I had to confess I hadn't tried any of this before. The course was new. It was a draft. We were failing.

She left unsatisfied, but I had a grin on my face. It might be my last semester, but my students were still failing to write and I was still failing to teach. We all had the benefits of instructive failure. I will never learn to teach or write; I will always fail and for that I am forever grateful.

Behind the Culture Shocks

DANLING FU

Three years ago, I began to teach undergraduate students in this country. I thought I was well equipped to teach, as I had seven years' experience teaching college students in China. In addition, I had spent four years researching in American classrooms from elementary to high school and two years teaching courses to practicing teachers in this country. But my first university teaching position in America was a real cultural shock.

Bound by my previous experience teaching Chinese college students, I was not used to the ways that American students reacted to learning and instructors. I was especially shocked by their questioning, negotiating, and bargaining with instructors about their grades. With my Chinese cultural background, I expected students who were not pleased with grades to ask me in what way they could improve their work in order to receive better grades, not question my grading system and blame me for not giving them fair grades. I expected the students faithfully to follow the instructor's requirements and work harder than the instructor requested, especially the ones who were not pleased with the grades they received. When the students didn't react as I expected, I became very frustrated, and this frustration became more and more overwhelming as the semester went on.

I stumbled through that first year with constant shocks and frustrations. In order to make students discuss what I expected them to in their papers, I was determined to make each assignment as specific as possible. I decided to adopt some kind of point grading system. My intention was to force students to work hard and to have less space to question and bargain with me about their grades.

The second year, I put a lot of effort into writing step-by-step guidelines for each assignment—sometimes two whole pages of questions—and working out a complicated and concrete grading system. For instance, I would deduct points if a paper missed an appropriate transition between paragraphs or if it didn't start or end properly. I would take more points off if students didn't support their ideas with specific examples and present them in a logical way. I used what students cared about most, grades, as the tool to try to manage my class, to motivate students to work hard, and to gain control over my teaching.

Nevertheless, few students improved. Instead, more of them became confused. My step-by-step instructions, instead of guiding students' writing, restricted their thinking. And when they followed the guidelines strictly, their writing became choppy and lacked cohesion. Though I stressed in a footnote, "Please don't answer the questions provided here step-by-step, otherwise your grades will suffer," that is what they did anyway. About 50 percent of students' writing was fragmented, lacked depth of thinking, or did not have a proper beginning or ending. Once I became so angry at the students that I took five points from every paper that was incohesive. Half of the class suffered. They figured out that with five points gone out of fifteen, they received a D. They all became outraged. Rather than motivating them to study harder, my grading system made the students care and worry more about grades. Many students showed little interest in the collaborative projects, which were not graded, and paid most attention to the graded assignments.

Grading became a tremendous burden on me as well. I spent more time figuring out the points a paper should get than conferring individually with students about their work. I not only had to count carefully the points for each paper but had to give my reasons for taking points off. Even then, many students still questioned even one point lost out of ten. When the students received their papers, they spent a long time counting the points they lost and converting the points they received to letter grades. It bothered me very much to see them be so concerned about grades but show such little interest in understanding what was wrong with their writing. To deal with this kind of attitude, I could do nothing but punish them with still lower grades.

Worst of all, I created a distance between me and my students. They were angry at me. They showed their anger not only by arguing about grades but also by arguing against whatever I presented in class. Their angry words still often ring in my ears today: "What Mrs. X said is different than what you say. Don't you think she knows more than you? She has been a principal for twenty-six years!" "We don't see the methods that you taught being done in our placement school; do you think you are really preparing us for the real world?" "What does my learning to write well have to do with teaching language arts to children?" "I think phonics programs work well, otherwise we all wouldn't be here." Some of their words fell like bombs: "Your evaluation system is ridiculous!" "Be specific with your assignments!" "No grades? No way! How do I know how I am doing in this course?" "Revise it? I don't know what you want!"

With a bunch of angry students like this, teaching became something I dreaded. Without the relationship, there was no real teaching and learning. I felt that I couldn't teach in this culture, that I would never get used to students who were so overconfident, disrespectful, and "democratic." The big blow was their end-of-the-year evaluations. My students gave me low "grades" too, and it hurt.

What was wrong with my teaching? Why didn't my strategies work? How could I learn to deal with American students better? I desperately sought solutions. I invited colleagues to observe my teaching and consulted with my students and mentors. They all tried to help. Some of their words struck me hard. My colleague Bess Altwerger advised me, "Don't expect that all students will immediately grasp the concepts we teach them, especially those they have never experienced or even heard of before. When we try to change their thinking, it takes time." My mentor Don Graves said to me, "Danling, remember your students are not too far from the high school students you studied, only two years older. What did you expect? If they didn't write enough in past school years, how can they suddenly write well in college? Please start where they are and look at their strengths."

"Start where students are and look at their strengths." I constantly preached this to my preservice students, but I failed to practice it in my own teaching. I realized that the shock I experienced from my American students came from my focus on what they couldn't do well and how they behaved differently from my expectations. Focusing on their weaknesses, I worked out ineffective strategies: providing detailed guidelines for their assignments and adopting a point grading system. The guidelines told students what they should say and in what order. The point grading system punished them if they didn't say or do what I expected them to. These two strategies not only prevented me from recognizing my students' strengths but also stripped them of their power as learners.

Examining the meaning behind my practices, I realized that I used grades as my way to control the students and as magic tools to push the students to learn. I forced them to pay attention to grades but not to actual learning. At the same time, I trapped myself in a grade-dominant system. Bothered by the students' arguments with me about grades, I created an overly specific system, which I thought would allow the least possible room for argument. In doing this, I demonstrated further to my students that grades were not only important but also powerful and controlled their learning. In my book *My Trouble Is My English* (1995), I used the learning experiences of four youngsters as cases to show how our students' learning is controlled by the grading system used in American schools. In my teaching, I fell into the same teaching model and system I criticized.

Thinking back on my teaching practice during those first two years, I realize that my students must have been experiencing cultural shock as well. I wonder why I never considered that it was the first time they'd had a professor with a foreign accent, an instructor from China who was preparing them to be teachers in this country. They must have been overwhelmed by my unfamiliar expectations and strange behavior. I complained about them because they were so unfamiliar but failed to see things from their perspective. If I had taken into consideration the shocks they might experience from my teaching, I would have adjusted my methods and expectations. On the contrary, I expected them to adjust to my ways of teaching. One of the important qualities of being a successful teacher is to decenter oneself—to think from the students' perspective and adjust one's teaching style to their ways of learning. Certainly in my first two years of teaching, I failed to practice the theory I preached.

It took me three years to learn to look beyond the strangeness and unfamiliarity of my American students, to understand and recognize the beauty of their values, the uniqueness in their learning style, and their special ways of knowing. When I focused on my students' weaknesses, I was constantly overwhelmed. Instead of helping them learn, I put my efforts into protecting myself from their arguments. By using grades as power, I set myself up as an opposing force. But when I placed less stress on grades, I truly freed my students to take risks and feel less frustrated in their learning. My students started to find joy in their learning. And teaching became joyous to me as well. In the past three years of teaching in this culture, my students have opened my mind and taught me how to teach them from their ways of learning. We have provided each other with many multicultural experiences as we have adjusted and responded to each other in our goal of learning to teach together.

It Silly 'Cuz It Silly: A Story of Beginning to Teach

JANE TOWNSEND

What rocked my complacency and preconceptions about teaching and learning was a group of multicolored high school seniors who had all failed English once before. It was my first day of formal teaching, I had already conscientiously learned each student's name, and I was determined to be innovative, engaging, and hip. My assumption about English study—built on my own successful school career—was that the whole class would share a reading, we'd then discuss it thoughtfully, and finally, each student would write an essay. My students were mostly poor, mostly blacks and Hispanics. They'd resided on the edges of society's privilege all their lives. They were used to filling in blanks on mimeographed sheets and passing the time. I wanted to make a difference in their lives. I wanted to help.

I was told to teach a lesson on persuasion, and I decided to bring in music—I was going to do something new. It was the early seventies, Vietnam War protests were in *my* air, so I chose Bob Dylan's "Subterranean Homesick Blues," a song that stirred *my* soul. I made a copy of the lyrics for each student, borrowed a portable stereo, and with nervous excitement began class. Standing in front of rows of students, I passed out song sheets and broadcast the music. When Dylan's last guttural chord had faded, I looked expectantly at a sea of still faces, and my knees began to wobble. "So," I said. "What do you think?" No one responded (probably not a question they'd been asked often). My legs began to shake. "Uh, I'd just like to know what you think of the song," I coaxed with a smile and a sinking heart. Blank faces. My body began a full-scale, dreadful tremor. More silence.

Finally, when I thought my heart must burst from apprehension, a large black girl in the back of the room—Amanda Lee Cannon, a young woman I'll always remember—leaned back in her chair and languidly raised her hand. My heart leapt with hope. "Amanda Lee," I said, nodding encouragement in her direction, "what did you think?" Amanda Lee took her time and casually remarked, "I think it silly." "Oh," I gushed, hardly stopping to think about the import of what she was saying. "Um, gosh, that's interesting. Tell me, um, what makes you say that? Uh, tell me more." Amanda Lee looked me in the eye, stretched out her large, lean body, and replied, "I think it silly 'cuz it silly." And with that, she folded her ebony arms on the desk and put her head down. While I gaped, in a desperate dawning, one head after another went down. And I stood facing a class of students who said no with a firmness and a power that changed my teaching life forever.

I've blacked out the rest of that day's class. I can remember driving home in tears, wondering how I'd find the courage to return the next day and feeling certain that teaching was not the job for me. I'm not sure what made me begin to think of the incident from my students' point of view rather than wallowing in my own angst. If I wanted to energize these students, I knew I'd have to do something very different from what I'd expected teaching to be. I knew that these students had long ago—for many different reasons—been pushed or inadvertently shoved to the sidelines of school. Why they put their heads down with common determination, why they didn't just humor me with empty responses, I don't know. Maybe they sensed I *wanted* to do right. They didn't expect much from school, but neither did they want to coddle some do-gooding white liberal talking about issues and ideas that had no apparent, real connection to their lives. If I wanted to help them feel the electrifying potential of reading and writing and talking, I'd have to find ways to begin with *their* concerns, *their* souls.

So, the next day I came in with more music—but this time, Jimi Hendrix's song "Changes," which I hoped would signal my intention. And, again with my knees shaking, I organized an activity that I'd heard about in a methods class (possibly the only useful idea from that whole course). I was breathless with anxiety as I walked around the room with an envelope full of folded-up pieces of paper. I asked each student to select a paper from the envelope, read what it said, and not show it to anyone else. "Then," I announced, "when I begin to play the music, follow the instructions on your paper." What I'd written on these pieces of paper were mostly the small, forbidden acts of classroom life: make a paper airplane and fly it around the room, walk around shaking different people's hands, draw on the blackboard, stand at your desk and count backward from one hundred, write a note to a friend, and so on. Each student had a different task to do. After saying that they were to freeze when I stopped the music, I turned on the record player and Jimi Hendrix started to groove. Chaos reigned for a few minutes as each student blossomed into movement. Then I turned off the music and told the students to sit back down. The kids had been having a big time, dancing around, talking, and laughing, but they sat down and turned curious faces toward me—a very different set of faces from the previous day's—wondering what might be next.

I asked them to write down everything they'd seen while the music played, and the fascinating trick was that those who'd been moving around the room, interacting with other people, had seen far more, had indeed much longer lists, of what had been happening than had the students who sat at their desks or turned their backs to the room while at the board. Spontaneously, we began having a spirited discussion about the benefits of travel, open minds, observation. By *talking*—listening to different points of view, hearing one another's stories, finding common ground—we began to establish a sense of working together to stretch our understanding. I was certainly stretching mine. "Let's do it again, Miss! Let's do it again!" the chorus of student voices resounded. I knew then that teaching wasn't going to be easy, but it was possible.

Oops!

JILL OSTROW

I was sitting at a large table surrounded by principals, assistant principals, and teachers from my school district. It was the last meeting of our language arts curriculum group. I remember seeing someone come into the large conference room and whisper something in the ear of our assistant superintendent. I watched her as she slipped quietly out of the room. She returned about twenty minutes later and chose to sit in the empty chair next to me. My assistant principal leaned over to her and the question he asked, which I overheard, made me sink slowly down into my soft conference-room chair.

"You didn't happen to just have a meeting with a man in a red hat who drives a big red truck, did you?" he asked her with a smile on his face. She looked at him, then me, and as the blood suddenly left my face, I heard her say, very sarcastically, "Why, yes. How did you know!" I knew then that the little meeting she was called away to had to do with my classroom and me.

My difficulty over the years working in a public school has not been the lack of money, the curriculum guides, or the growing class size; it has been the fire marshal.

My classroom is built from the children's imaginations. We build structures, display work on walls, and bring in comfortable furniture to sit on. The physical environment is crucial to my philosophy of how children learn. Apparently, the fire marshal disagrees with this philosophy!

Putting butcher paper up across the walls is a no-no. We have a rule in our building, put in place by the fire marshal, that pieces of work displayed or tacked on the wall need to be at least two feet apart. Two feet? That would allow me to put up work from about four children!

One year we made a village of huts out of carpet roll tubes and butcher paper. We all prayed the fire marshal wouldn't decide to make a surprise visit during the time we had the village up. He did come one time that year to tell me that the work that was displayed on the walls outside the classroom was too close together. I seemed to be getting a name within my school as the "fire marshal's target." He did tend to visit my room more regularly than the other rooms.

The kids were very aware of the fire marshal. His visits, or should I say his interrogations, were something they came to expect. I started noticing how they would use the fire marshal in their stories. They would write about the "mean" fire marshal, and he was often the "bad guy" in superhero stories. He became a sort of negative mascot. We would often build something and someone would call out, "Just wait until the fire marshal sees this!"

The fire marshal never did see the village huts; however, the following year, when we built the island hut and palm trees, he arrived with a vengence.

Funny, but what the fire marshal had a problem with was the butcher paper on the walls, not the hut in the middle of the room made out of carpet roll tubes or the palm trees with leaves hanging over the light fixtures.

He blustered into my room one day, very rudely I might add, and gave me one day to remove the butcher paper covering the hut roof and the butcher paper on the walls. He didn't tell me this directly, mind you; he told the district maintenance person he was with. He never looked directly at me. I asked him why he saw the butcher paper as being such a hazard, and he launched into a lengthy description of what would happen if a flaming fire were to spread through our room. He also looked down at me and told me that "any child that held a lighter to the paper would start a fire that would spread so fast you wouldn't know what hit you." He said it in way that sounded like *anyone* would know that.

"What are you talking about?" I said, seething with irritation. "I have six-, seven-, and eight-year-olds. They aren't bringing lighters to school!"

"Anyone could come in here with a flammable implement. The paper comes down," was his irritating answer. I was fuming as I looked up at his unsmiling face. I wanted to yell at him and tell him to look at me.

"Wait, are you telling me that the palm trees that are hanging over the light fixtures and the carpet roll tubes all over the room are fine, but the butcher paper on the walls isn't?"

"Yes, the rolls are okay," he told me, his back to me, as he was walking out the door.

"Do you understand that this is a *school?* Do you understand how important it is to put up the work of the children?" I tried to explain to his retreating figure.

He turned his head and snapped back at me, "I don't think you need to have this much stuff on the walls or in your room in order for them to learn."

Okay, so here was the fire marshal telling me about how children learn? I sighed, and muttered under my breath, then turned around. I realized that all the kids in the room had heard the encounter. Needless to say, they were not happy with his decision.

Later that day, as the kids and I were reading, we saw flashes of light. I had one of the kids go to the door to see who it was. Mr. Fire Marshal was back, but this time he was taking pictures of the room through the doorway. Something told me it wasn't because he liked my room so much that he wanted to remember it! I walked over and asked if he'd come back after school, since he had already disturbed my class twice today. He turned his six-foot body around and left with a very annoying smirk on his face. I was angry, but I also felt my stomach twist into a nervous knot. Even though I knew this guy was a pain and totally out of line, I knew he felt the same about me.

That was the morning of the language arts meeting. That was the day that my assistant superintendent informed me that if my room wasn't "up to code" the school would be shut down. Wow! I almost got my school closed—all because of butcher paper!

When the fire marshal threatens to close a school, what power do *I* have? I changed my tactics; I learned over the years to "work" with him. I only use flameproof paper now, or I use flameproof fabric. It is easier to get around the rules than fight an unbeatable fight.

If the butcher paper was cause to shut the school down, the six-foot-by-ten-foot hill and mountain structure we were planning to build out of chicken wire and papier mâché I figured would shut the entire district down! So, instead of waiting for a confrontation, I decided to talk to the fire marshal beforehand. Great decision on my part. It was apparent that he liked being the one to come to with questions. He told me our structure would be fine if we mixed some baking soda with the papier mâché and sprayed the entire structure with fire-resistant spray. Now, I always keep a bottle of that handy and spray practically everything!

As for the school that next day after my language arts meeting? It wasn't shut down, but I never did get a chance to look at those pictures he took.

Time Out: Lessons from "Playing School"

BOBBI FISHER

In my classroom, as my first graders finish their daily writing, they meander over to the rug area to read, either with friends or by themselves. The flow feels extremely comfortable and natural as part of our reading/writing classroom. Reading includes reading Big Books, little predictable books, trade books, magazines, songs and poems, as well as telling stories with puppets, listening to a story tape, *and* playing school.

Playing school is one of the most popular choices. The number of participants varies from two to six children, all of whom collectively work out the rules for taking turns being teacher and student. The chosen teacher sits on my chair by the teaching easel and, regardless of reading sophistication, exudes confidence as he or she takes my pointer and leads the students in song from a chart or initiates the reading of a Big Book. The students, at their usual place on the floor, sing or read along and willingly participate when asked to locate or notice something in the text.

I love to glance over and observe the natural learning classroom modeled in dynamic action. The "teacher" takes on my role as he or she demonstrates what I do during shared literacy. The students role-play themselves as participants. They all are performing for themselves. Watching the children play school enables me to assess what they are learning from my daily demonstrations of literacy strategies, as well as observe our classroom community in action.

But one day while observing a group of children playing school, I didn't like what I saw. As Danielle looked at Kathryn and pointed away from the group area, I heard her kindly but firmly say, "Please go to time-out." I knew there was only one person who could have provided the model for this demonstration—me. The children were practicing being like me and I didn't like what they were practicing.

Another day soon after that Peter was being extremely silly during shared literacy time, making faces and trying to engage the other children in his "game." As we read *The Little Yellow Chicken,* a favorite Big Book by Joy Cowley, his behavior began to distract me. Undoubtedly the children could sense my frustration because someone piped up with the suggestion, "Why don't you send him to time-out?" I must have been using time-out more than I realized.

Seeing time-out from this perspective hit me hard and helped me re-evaluate why I use it. I had sensible arguments to support my use of time-out. I saw it as a way to help children choose to be responsible for their own learning and behavior when they are disrupting the group. But time-out is initiated, structured, and controlled by adults, not by children. For the most part adults decide what is disruptive. Children don't really have the choice whether to participate or not.

I know that children don't really want to leave the group. They want to be a full member of the classroom club, and it is my responsibility as a teacher to give them free and open membership. When I ask a child to go to time-out, or even if a child "chooses" to take time-out, our classroom community is broken. We are not all together. Someone is missing and separated from us. I am reminded of Vivian Paley's discussion of the time-out chair in *The Boy Who Would Be a Helicopter* (1986). "Being locked up seldom helped a child not do something, though it did notify everyone that the child was bad" (p. 88).

Looking back on other instances in my classroom, I see how time-out deprives children of control of their own learning because it fosters academic and social competition. The children begin to vie for teacher approval, using it as their main gauge of success. Extrinsic motivation takes dominance over intrinsic motivation as they choose between pleasing the teacher and joining the time-out game or using their own inner resources to guide their learning. The two aren't mutually inclusive. As Alfie Kohn states in *Punished by Rewards* (1993), "No strategy for classroom management can hope to be effective in the long term if it ignores the fact that misbehavior often reflects students' lack of interest in much of what we are teaching" (p. 217).

Although time-out may be a short-term solution for teacher control, it is not a viable strategy to help children understand and control their behavior. When Paley eliminated the time-out chair for good, she told the children, "You'll all have to learn to act properly without the time-out chair. In fact, without any punishment at all. I'm tired of punishing people. It makes children sad and it makes me sad too" (p. 89).

Time-out makes me sad, because it breaks down classroom community and encourages the children to compete rather than learn together. I'm grateful to my students for helping me see how using this practice has been a failure for all of us. I plan to give up using time-out. Our society is replete with people ostracized from various groups who feel they are not a part of any community. If I can't make the commitment to every one of the children I teach that they can trust me to give them full and unconditional membership in the class, then I am cutting them off from the possibility of full membership in society.

It's difficult to change the educational practices that have been so useful and acceptable to us, and doubts and concerns will arise. I know there will be times when I'm tempted to take the easy and expedient way out and say, "Time-out." But I hope I'll be able to "just say no" to time-out and keep my classroom an inclusive community for all.

References

Cowley, Joy. 1988. *The Little Yellow Chicken*. Bothell, WA: The Wright Group.

Kohn, Alfie. 1993. *Punished by Rewards: The Trouble with Gold Stars, Incentive Plans, A's, Praise, and Other Bribes*. Boston: Houghton Mifflin.

Paley, Vivian. 1986. *The Boy Who Would Be a Helicopter: The Uses of Storytelling in the Classroom*. Chicago: University of Chicago Press.

One Long Line

C A R Y L   H U R T I G

I cannot touch the earth until I learn

to use my personal gifts of heart,

sight, touch, taste, smell and hearing.

Calvin Hecocta

As I was driving to Powell's Bookstore in downtown Portland, Oregon, a white van cut in front of me. Emblazoned on its side in clean blue letters were the words "ODS Health Care: Trust Us With Your Health." Leaning forward with squinted eyes to identify the driver, this representative of my health's future, I caught a glimpse of the guy as he gunned the van through a yellow light; he was smoking. Laughing out loud, I had a moment of identification. Students enroll in my classes not realizing that at times I'm the driver of this van, a bit out of control and smoking like a madwoman, dangerous to myself and all on board.

In no area do I feel more like this smoking, speeding driver than when I approach diversity issues. So often in teaching, we place ourselves in expert positions when our knowing is superficial, gleaned from fragments of information picked up in books. As a skinny white woman raised in a segregated southern California suburb, ethnic diversity is something I passionately want to understand but have had limited experience with.

For several summers I've worked for a program called the Oregon Governors' School for Citizen Leadership, a residential program for high school students that explores issues of diversity, racism, gender, and leadership. The program is difficult to explain, since it's about transformation; it's a messy process, with more loose ends than I care to think about. As members of the learning community, staff members learn at least as much as the students through the intensity and chaos of it all. Rupert Sheldrake, in relating the new theories in science to his understanding of the nature of work, claims physics suggests that all life comes from the original fireball, made up of atoms alive and dancing, not dead matter as previously assumed, so our work should be full of wonder, surprise, and chaos (Fox 1994). Well, the Governors' School has no problem in these departments!

63

This is a story about chaotic and naked teaching, a time I experienced a sense of failure.

During the institute there is an overnight at Opal Creek in the Oregon Cascades, a retreat center in the heart of one of the few remaining old-growth timber stands. On staff we have a First Nation counselor, Calvin Hecocta, who teaches about leadership and the environment and provides opportunities for students to experience sweat lodges and other aspects of his culture. We take the students to Opal Creek to introduce them to the beauty of a virgin forest, establish a connection to nature from which we can explore environmental issues, and undertake a physical ordeal intended to build community. At 6 A.M. seventy teens and staff members pile into pickup trucks to bounce and careen our way up a narrow, rock-paved road to the trail head, from there to hike fifteen miles up a cascade trail to Whetstone Mountain, a plateau that once served as a First Nation vision quest site. It now looks out over a vista of sharp, clear-cut mountain peaks, at once sickening and beautiful. One cannot sit on Whetstone Mountain and fail to be in awe of how humans can cut down forests for profit (toilet paper, computer paper); one cannot help but wonder at the complete stupidity of this act. A student noted that if they used toilet paper in India, there would be no trees left in the world. I have never forgotten that.

Most of the teens on this hike were city kids, and many of them had never placed a sneaker on a forest floor, nor exercised much, for that matter. I'm certain many of them had not known what it felt like to love a special tree, nor noticed a sweet fern growing on the bark of a fir trunk split open by lightening. As you can imagine, this group did not know how to enter the forest with reverence. Calvin later talked to us about asking permission to enter the forest.

As we often do when approaching chaos and taking risks with students, the staff overdosed on rules, the main one being that the group must stay in one long line, all seventy of us, tripping, slinking, scraping our way straight up an almost invisible mountain path. It was a very slow hike. The intent of this policy was safety and community building, both honorable goals. I'm still not sure that we were "wrong" but we did pay a price for following our one-line rule.

The one-line policy meant that the healthier hikers had to slow down and watch the ones having difficulty. You might be thinking this isn't all bad, and it's not. Over time we started helping each other, not only thinking, Can I make it? but considering the person in front and back, offering help when possible. And still, many struggled. For example, one staff member, who was fifty pounds overweight, almost passed out from the effort of climbing the mountain. She claims, looking back, that she's never been so humiliated in her life, enduring complaints about her pace and comments about her weight that were "whispered" behind her back. She probably would have preferred privacy to "community" at this point. Several of the students on the hike twisted ankles, had asthma attacks, and other physical challenges. Staying together exaggerated their difficulties in front of a large audience; often they were ridiculed, as can happen in the adolescent world of cruel honesty and rough edges.

Some of the more athletic wanted to practically run up the mountain. Staying together was particularly frustrating for them, and they organized a rebellion so they could split off and hike ahead. One staffer had to call a halt and facilitate a special conference to slow them down so we could stay together. (How often does that happen in education?) It worked, for a while, but this raises painful questions. We don't all experience the hike in the same way, because of what we bring to the trail head, but so often we insist on doing the same hike together, with many people feeling they have to leave much of themselves behind or they are somehow deficient. Is it right to lead students to a place where they encounter their vulnerabilities? Isn't that education at its best? Where is the line between growing edge and humiliation? What elements make the difference between a place to grow versus a place to know shame about our limits? And who says how fast the hike is paced anyway? I don't have easy answers for these questions. I do know I need a lot of support to be willing to face these places in myself, but the times I do, I learn the most.

After we reached the top of Whetstone Mountain and silently ate our lunches, feeling a brief sense of victory and accomplishment in making it to the top, our First Nation staff member, Calvin Hecocta, publicly announced that he planned to take a select group of male students to a special vision quest site to engage in a coming-of-age ceremony. I find myself very uncomfortable even writing about this because I'm afraid of revealing my own unknowing. It's painful to realize that most culture is unconscious, as are biases, and while I feel that I'm not prejudiced, that I care about all people, I also sense that this isn't quite true, since culture is mostly hidden from us; it is a bit like a dream we live and remember but don't know how to interpret. Secretly, I realize I don't even know much about my own cultural roots and behaviors, let alone someone else's.

As you may have guessed, the white hike leaders, including myself, said no to Calvin's separating from the group. It didn't seem fair to the students not offered the opportunity, we worried about keeping track of everyone, but mostly it was just too spontaneous; it didn't fit our plan. It broke up the line. We were going to Stay in Community. The boys denied this truly unique and unrepeatable opportunity were outraged. Calvin was furious with the white staff members. At that time, in my mind, staying together was the right thing to do, although I felt quite uneasy and was angry that Calvin had "put us" in this position. This was clearly a cultural conflict, but what did it mean? When discussing this with Calvin later, he told me that this group of boys he selected had been meeting individually with him throughout the institute, expressing interest in vision quests, and he had promised them to take them to the site if there was a chance. We didn't know this.

Other times during the institute, Calvin protested that we wanted to use him for prayers during scheduled activities, in a planned way. His preference and leadership style was to respond when he sensed a need arise, and he expected us to trust him that he would do the work at this level when appropriate. By putting him on stage during ceremonies, I suspect he felt like the token Indian, proving the program's commitment to diversity. Perhaps he did not understand our dominant white culture orientation to sticking to plans and controlling the time, just as we failed to comprehend his spirit-guided leadership style. The skillful choice would have been to sit down and work this out, putting everyone's needs on the table, but, sadly, we were not fully aware of the conflict as we experienced it, as is so often the case. There were seventy people needing to finish the hike. Real cultural conflicts happen on this level, when we have to make hard decisions, under pressure, with opposing yet equally valid values, styles, and cultures meeting head-on. What do you do? Take turns?

So we started down the mountain after our confrontation; about twenty minutes later the group slowed to concentrate on a sound in the trees. At first I thought it might be an animal, it seemed so haunting. Listening, I whispered to myself, It's Calvin, and squatted on the trail. He had gone to the vision quest site alone and was offering songs and prayers that filled the forest with a mournful wail, a reverent prayer, a holy encounter. It broke my heart. The entire group sat down where they had stood to listen silently. It was one of the few times when we truly experienced community.

There is a small lake by my home, which is drained for three months each winter, so that docks can be propped up and repaired. As I walked by it today, observing the water recede, I welcomed these months of emptiness, when the jagged bottom rocks are visible. There needs to be an empty place of nonactivity in my life to consider what has come before. Three years have passed since this hike; emptiness, time, and study have taught me much about our long line up the mountain, and it still hurts to write about it, so there is more to learn. I'm grateful I took the hike. Like most painful experiences, the times I "fail" teach me the most, remind me of my limits and unknowing. I feel guilty that my learning had to come at someone's expense. This is part of the tension of diversity work. Caring isn't enough. I also need to study and understand my own culture and the diverse cultures around me. But I suspect a hike will always entail blisters and bruises, a certain requirement of putting up with one another's limits, tripping over one another's shoes. Maybe that's how it's supposed to be.

It has become a cliché to say, We teach what we need to learn. I ask myself what possessed me to become a teacher addressing diversity issues. What an impostor. I'm the van driver who hasn't passed the driving test. Yet we cannot truly know ourselves or one another without understanding culture, and the only way to do so is to continue to approach the mountain together.

The mountain is changing too. The first year we took the hike, we could drink safely from the streams bubbling up from underground rivers, fed by icy mountain snow. This year the Opal Creek hike docent told us it was not safe to drink from these streams anymore. They may make you sick. We can't afford to focus only on human respect. Calvin reminded us at the end of the hike that the trees, the mountain path, the rocks, and the ferns are our ancestors too, and that learning to enter the woods reverently is absolutely tied to the survival of the human race.

Reference

Fox, Matthew. 1994. *The Reinvention of Work: A New Vision of Livelihood for Our Time*. San Francisco: HarperCollins.

New-Teacher Blues: How I Survived My First Year

BILL BIGELOW

It was Friday afternoon. The end of my sixth-period freshman social studies class. As two of my students walked out the door, I overheard as one turned to the other and said, "Do you know what this class reminds me of? A local TV commercial."

It was a crushing comment. I knew exactly what she meant. As hard as I was working, the class still felt ragged, amateurish—well intended but sloppy. Her metaphor, invoking the image of a salesman trying too hard, was perfect. As the last student filed out, the best I could do was remember the words of Lee Hays of The Weavers, "Like kidney stones and the Nixon presidency, this too will pass."

First Jobs

It was late October before I got my first teaching job—at Grant High School in Portland, Oregon. The school enrolled a diverse student body, about 30 percent African American, the European American students drawn from both working class and "up on the ridge" neighborhoods. I had two preps: U.S. history and something called "freshman social studies" (and baseball coaching in the spring). As I was to learn, I'd been hired to teach "overflow" classes, classes that had been formed because Grant's enrollment was higher than expected. Teachers chose "surplus" students to donate to these new classes. Then administrators hired a sub to baby-sit while they sought permission to offer a contract to a regular teacher. In the meantime, the kids drove two subs to quit. I was hired during the tenure of sub number three.

My first meeting with the principal and vice principal was perfunctory. They told me that "freshman social studies" meant one semester career education, one semester world geography, and no, they weren't sure which came first. But I could pick up my two-ream allotment of ditto paper from the department chair. They gave me a key to Room 10 and sent me to review "my work station," as the principal, an ex-Navy man, called it. Room 10 was a runt: a tiny basement classroom, crammed with 1950s-style student desks and a loud, hulking heating unit in the rear; but it was mine.

Don't Be a Lone Ranger

Before the students, came the questions: Should I use textbooks? How do I grade? What kind of "discipline" policy should I have? How should I arrange the classroom? What do I teach on the first day? My answers to these and other typical first-year questions are less important than the process of answering them. And this is perhaps the most valuable lesson I drew from that first year: don't be a lone ranger. In September I had organized a study/support group with several teachers, some brand new, others with a few years' experience. We were united by a vision of creating lively, thoughtful classrooms in which we provoked students to question the roots of social problems and encouraged them to believe they could make a difference. This group became my haven, offering comfort in times of stress—which was most of the time—and concrete advice on vexing questions.

Occasionally, our meetings turned into aimless whining sessions. But other times, a simple comment could remind us of our ideals and keep us on the path. I remember in a weak moment confessing that I was just too tired, scrambling to create my own curriculum from scratch, retyping excerpts from assorted books (those were the days before teachers were allowed access to copy machines), and that I was going to start relying on the textbook. My friend Peter Thacker, sympathetic yet disapproving, asked, "Bill, do you really want to do that?" It may have bordered on guilt trip, but that's all it took for me to remember that in fact I really *didn't* want to do that. The group was simultaneously collective conscience and inspiration.

I don't mean to imply that all textbooks are so wretched. But as a beginning teacher I needed to see myself as a producer, not merely a consumer, of curriculum. It's hard work to translate the world into engaging lesson plans, but unless we're content to subordinate our classrooms to the priorities of the corporations that produce textbooks and other canned curriculums, that's exactly what we have to do every day. It's not that textbooks are a vast wasteland of corporate propaganda, but they can easily narrow and misdirect our efforts. To offer just one example, in Jim Loewen's (1995) critique of contemporary U.S. history textbooks he demonstrates that all major texts downplay or totally ignore the history of the struggle against racism in the United States. Especially as a beginning teacher, if I had relied on textbooks to shape the outlines of my U.S. history curriculum, I would have neglected crucial areas of inquiry—and may never have realized it.

Oral Sex and the Vice Principal

It began with a call asking me to report to the vice principal's office. The voice at the other end indicated it was urgent. The call gave me the creeps. From the moment we met, I'd felt that Lloyd Dixon, curriculum v.p., could look deep into my soul—and that he didn't like what he saw. When we passed in the hall he smiled thinly but with a glance that said, I've got your number, Bigelow. Although, I confess my classroom difficulties made me a tad paranoid.

Dixon's secretary ushered me into his office when I arrived. "It seems we have a problem, Bill." He paused to look at me and make sure I was duly appreciative of the serious nature of the meeting. "The mother of a student of yours, Dorothy Jennings, called to say that you had given Dorothy smutty material, a book that discusses oral sex. What's the story?"

I explained to the vice principal that the "smutty" material was Studs Terkel's *Working,* a book that included interviews with dozens of people—auto workers, hotel clerks, washroom attendants, musicians—who described what they did for a living and how they felt about it. I told him that it was a text the school had purchased and that I issued it to my ninth graders for some in-class reading during our career education study.

"Well, Bill, Dorothy apparently took the book home. And her mother's upset because of a section Dorothy read her about a prostitute, where she describes having oral sex."

I told him I had not assigned that chapter and that students didn't have permission to take the books home, as I taught two sections of the class but had only thirty-five copies of the book. I didn't mention that I had indeed considered using the chapter "Roberta Victor, Hooker" because it was filled with insights about sexism, law, and hypocrisy. The alleged oral sex description was a brief reference in a long interview. He ordered me to bring him a copy of *Working* so that he could read the passages I assigned and to meet with him again the next day. "You should be aware that I regard this as a serious situation," he said. And with that, New Teacher was waved out the door.

I went to see Tom McKenna, a fellow Grant teacher and member of my support group. Tom suggested I talk to our union rep. My visit with Thurston Ohman, a bighearted man with an easy, from-the-belly laugh, was a revelation. "You haven't done anything wrong," he assured me. "If they try to come after you in some way, the union will back you one hundred percent." It was a delicious moment, and I realized how utterly alone I'd felt up until that point. Ironically, in my classes we'd recently studied the rise of labor unions, but until that instant I'd never personally been a beneficiary of the "injury to one is an injury to all" solidarity.

Buoyed by my talk with Thurston, I returned to Vice Principal Dixon's office the next day. He wasn't worried about Mrs. Jennings anymore. But he was still upset. "Bill, I read over the pieces that you assigned. Very interesting. Pretty negative stuff. Do you know that the reading on the autoworker uses the s word five times and the f word once?"

"The s word?"

"Yes. On pages 258, 259, 261 and twice on page 262. The f word is used on page 265."

I didn't want to laugh, but I didn't know what to say. His complaint was about an interview with Gary Bryner, president of the United Auto Workers local at the Lordstown, Ohio, General Motors plant. I suspected that Dixon's ire was aimed more at Bryner's hard-hitting critique of the plant's deadening working conditions and his descriptions of workers' resistance—"negative stuff"—than at his occasional use of s and f words, but this wasn't the time to argue politics. "I guess I didn't realize, Mr. Dixon."

"No. Well, Bill, here's what I'd like you to do. Get a black marker and every time this gentleman uses the s and f words, darken them so students won't be exposed to that kind of language. Will you do that for me, Bill?"

I know some people would have fought it. Had it not been my first year as a teacher—a temporary teacher, no less—*I* would have fought. Instead I made one of those compromises that we're not proud of but that we make so we can live to fight another day. After school, magic marker in hand, I cleansed Gary Bryner of his foul language—in all thirty-five copies of *Working*.

I offer this instance of curricular censorship as a way of acknowledging that administrative repression can be a factor limiting the inventiveness of a first-year teacher. But in my experience, the intrusions of the Lloyd Dixons of the world are exceptions that prove the rule. And the rule is that we have an enormous amount of freedom. Even as a first-year teacher, the Jennings affair was my only brush with administrative censure. I frequently brought in controversial guest speakers, films, and additional readings. It was the year of Three Mile Island, the final months of the Sandinista revolution in Nicaragua, and a growing U.S. awareness of the injustices of South African apartheid. In class, we studied all of these. No doubt, it's important for individuals early in their teaching careers, as well as those of us further along, to make an assessment of the political context in which we work. After all, if we lose our job, we don't do anyone any good. But generally, I believe the most powerful agent of censorship lives in our own heads; we almost always have more freedom than we use.

Incidentally, I never met Mrs. Jennings. But she left her mark. For a long time I subconsciously imagined a Mrs. Jennings sitting at every student's home, hoping for a chance to chew me out for some teaching crime I'd committed: You snake, why'd you use that book-film-article-poem with my innocent child? In my imagination, parents were potential opponents, not allies, and I avoided calling them to talk about their children or what I was trying to teach. This neglect was a bad habit to fall into. Even from a narrow classroom-management standpoint, my failure to call home from time to time made my quest for classroom order a lonely campaign. Parents could have exerted a bit of pressure on the homefront. But they also could have told me something about their child, offered a fuller portrait than the one I

71

saw in my daily slice of forty-seven minutes. And that would likely have made me a more effective teacher.

The principal made his only appearance in my classroom on March 15. Actually, he didn't come in but knocked on the door and, when I answered, handed me my official termination notice. It was expected; I'd known I wouldn't be back because I was temporary, but still there had been that slight hope. I guess by contract or law March 15 was the final date to notify teachers if they wouldn't be returning. I had about three months to let my unemployment sink in.

When that June date finally came, I packed my little white Toyota with the files, books, posters, and other knickknacks I'd accumulated throughout the year. I stood looking at the bare walls, my tiny oak desk, and Hulk the heater. And I left. My tears didn't start until I was in the safety of my living room.

Tom McKenna had told me that at the end of the year he always felt like a jilted lover. Wait, there was more I wanted to say to you, he would think, as the students filed out for the last time. And, I always cared more about this than you did. Sitting there on my couch, I now knew exactly what he meant. When it's over, you're left with the should-have-dones, the sense of missed opportunities, and the finality of it all. The end-of-the-year cry has become one of my worklife rituals: There was more we had to say to each other.

References

Terkel, Studs. 1972. *Working*. New York: Avon.

Loewen, Jim. 1995. *Lies My Teacher Told Me*. New York: The New Press.

Messing Up in Science

PAT CORDEIRO

I took my title for this article from David Hawkins's title "Messing About in Science" (1974), an argument for the need to provide structured time for exploratory play/work in the learning process. But I've changed his "messing *about*" to the personally much more accurate "messing *up*."

Like David Hawkins, my school too had Elementary Science Study units, "ESS kits" we called them, and like Hawkins, I too studied firsthand my "young children's learning in science." Unlike Hawkins, who perhaps had more time for observation than I did, I came away convinced that "learning in science" was somewhat different than I had expected.

Take the year we did a prescribed unit called Mystery Powders.

That year I was teaching fourth grade, a class that started with twenty-seven students—a large class for our rural community—and grew midwinter to thirty-four. It was my first time teaching fourth grade, we had wall-to-wall desks, and this was right at the height of my dedication to exploring how to promote process learning. Plus that year I had the classic group of concerned parents, many of them of the back-to-basics philosophy and all of them vocally suspicious of questionably structured "process" learning.

But I was determined to continue my process teaching mission, and I launched into Mystery Powders about November. I had taken the kit from the large science closet in the hall and was pleased to find that it was largely intact or could easily be resupplied from the supermarket. Some of the ESS kits, like Batteries and Bulbs—another story—required substantial replenishment in the spring to prepare them for use the following school year, and sometimes the technical ingredients of the kits were best ordered directly from ESS.

But Mystery Powders was just what it sounded like, a collection of white powders to "mess around" with, do charting and graphing with, and set about making hypotheses supported by primary data. The kit came with lots of little containers, tubes, tiny scales, and a couple of packages of white powders left

73

over from previous years. Teachers in past usages had added equipment, like the scales, so the kit as it sat on the shelf had quite a generative feel to it. I had gone to the store (as the manual had instructed) and bought additional white powders—sugar, baking soda, salt, flour—nothing toxic (as the manual had suggested).

It took me quite a while on weekends to get ready for these science excursions. I'm not good at memorizing teacher's manuals, steps, and questions; I'm much better at generating curriculum as we go. But I was convinced that there was a "right" way to do this "messing about" and that probably I could master it if I studied hard enough.

So I read the manual from cover to cover, made notes and lists, charts and graphs, and sheets with places for students to record their presence, time spent, and activities at the "science center." I devised envelopes and containers for cards with instructions for various tests to determine which powder went with which descriptor. I set up a Mystery Powders table in the corner of our crowded classroom, arranged tiny containers of various unlabeled powders in rows at "stations," set up clipboards—with attached pencils—and charts of who, how, why, and what findings, and placed the cards with instructions for various experiments in the center of the table. Finally, I made a large cardboard title, Mystery Powders Science Center, in case my principal decided to observe me that week, and launched into the unit Monday morning.

We went about our usual day that Monday, and for a few days after, with writing time in the morning, then readers workshop, and on to math, with manipulatives for thirty or so, doing as well as we could. It was always pretty hectic and I was always busy, managing, organizing, mediating, initiating, and above all, facilitating, as we thought we should in those days. But I was happy—kids were publishing, reading real books and talking about them, working through the math curriculum scope and sequence. I didn't really pay much attention to how things were going at the science center, but then, I reasoned, this was supposed to be a learning center, somewhat "teacher-proof" and certainly self-sufficient. That area of the classroom was always in the corner of my eye, and once in a while kids would ask for more supplies. Sometimes I tidied up near the table, but I didn't really focus on the work-in-progress. Daily life swirled past the science center.

Toward the end of the week, I decided to check up on how things were going. Things didn't look at all the same as when I had set them up. My kids, in a true generative fashion, had rearranged the table to suit their own needs. The instruction cards were nowhere to be seen, and the clipboards and charts appeared to have been turned into miniature tabletops. White powders were everywhere, and there really was no way to tell if what was in one container was a pure powder or a blend of everything. The tiny scales were in use, with huge piles of white powder on each side so that the tiny pans rested on the table and the arms holding the pans were bent. The area for quantifying weight was smeared with what looked like white paste, and the graph paper was covered with piles of translucent flour glue like my mother once made to hold up wallpaper. I had to conclude that scientific methods were not at work.

Later my kids told me that, early on, Davey had eaten all the sugar, so that eliminated that powder from the study entirely. They said they really enjoyed "playing with the stuff and mixing things" and I was reminded of the Christmas when my cousin got a Perfume Factory as a present and we all spent the day happily mixing awful-smelling concoctions in my aunt's bedroom. Science it wasn't; fun it was.

My kids also finally told me about the real science investigation that had been going on under my nose, outside my control, all the time. Because we published cardboard-covered books during writing time, we had a bookmaking center that included ample supplies of rubber cement in quart containers, which needed to be poured into little jars with brushes, a messy ritual we prepared for and shared cooperatively under my supervision.

However, during recess, under the guise of going to the bathroom, kids would regularly visit the classroom to pour rubber cement onto the countertop to dry. Rubber cement, as you may know, becomes soft and rubbery, quite pliable, when it hardens. Later in class, after the goo had dried, someone would peel it off and make it into a ball that bounced like crazy. As proof, they showed me several rubber cement balls that already resided up in the light fixtures, totally outside the pale of my normal classroom surveillance. Worse yet, Sheena had made what they called a "*huge* rubber cement ball," holding their hands out to show me the extreme size, and she kept it at home under her bed.

At first I was discouraged. What was worse, they were all in on it. I had to take it as a kind of compliment that they told me about it at all, but it took me a while to come round to this. I did have to admit it was science. They had, as a class, furtively, subversively, and collaboratively studied the properties of matter. And they had learned a lot. Although they certainly had not mastered the ins and outs of the fine art of a scientific method, still they had devised experiments, carved out time to perform them, and used available resources. They had produced recognized experts in the field, performed controlled tests, developed and revised hypotheses, and shared and disseminated knowledge. They had reported their findings and were eager to continue.

I succumbed to science as children experience it. In later years I would hear that my students told their parents that "they didn't do science," probably because they never had a textbook labeled *science*. At least I hoped so.

I came away feeling that in spite of my best efforts, my students did achieve some of the primary goals I held for them, what Eleanor Duckworth (1986) calls "the collective creation of knowledge"—they certainly had that. They enriched their curiosity, furthered their understanding of the world around them, and experienced what Vygotsky (1986) calls "spontaneous and scientific concepts." Most important, they developed a persistent interest in science and experimentation. I decided that there was time enough for them later to learn the language of science, how to replicate classic experiments, and when to follow the scientific method. In developing their own sense of experiments, they had begun to construct an understanding of methodology, a personal set of steps that might guide them in coping with real-world problems in a way that training in laboratory experimentation might not.

As for fulfilling the multiple goals of the teacher's manual of Mystery Powders? I think we did accomplish many of them, although in a slightly different fashion than the curriculum developers intended. I came away sharing a continuing commitment with Hawkins and Duckworth to both the role of exploratory play/work in learning and the necessity for "collective construction" in creating knowledge in any area. But I decided that I should pay more attention to the source of David Hawkins's title and his concept for science education—the Kenneth Grahame classic *Wind in the Willows* and the words of the Water Rat: "'Believe me, my young friend, there is nothing—absolutely nothing—half so much worth as simply messing about in boats. Simply messing,' he went on dreamily, 'messing—about—in—boats—messing—.'"

References

Duckworth, Eleanor. 1986. *Inventing Density.* Grand Forks, ND: University of North Dakota Press.

Grahame, Kenneth. 1980. *Wind in the Willows.* New York: Henry Holt.

Hawkins, David. 1974. *The Informed Vision: An Essay on Science Education.* New York: Agathon Press.

Vygotsky, Lev. 1986. *Thought and Language.* Alex Kozulin, trans. and ed. Cambridge, MA: MIT Press.

Race Differences: A White Teacher and a Native Son

LEILA CHRISTENBURY

> *We had the experience but missed*
> *the meaning.*
>
> T. S. Eliot, *"The Dry Salvages,"*
> Four Quartets

O ne of the bitterest events of my teaching life involves a yearlong failure of communication between me and a student. Miguel saw English class as a political struggle and me, the white teacher, as his opponent. I saw English class as my lifework and Miguel as one of my many bright students. My rather feckless enthusiasm did not, however, win the day: Miguel and I ended up no closer together at the end of our year together. And to this day, I know I had the experience, but I'll be damned if I can tell anyone about the meaning.

It was a senior English class, my third year teaching at this high school, a large (two thousand students) urban institution with a strong racial mix (60 percent white, 40 percent African American) and a certain economic diversity (middle-class and working-class students).

I was deeply committed to two things: giving the students everything I had to offer and ensuring that the students took charge of their learning. For my part, I pulled out the stops. Once the class began, we voted on course content and negotiated assignments. Extended and student-designed projects and teacher/student negotiation were the norm.

Outside our class I also wanted to stretch our boundaries: as a group we went to a play, a local art museum, and a symphony concert—for almost all the students the first such events in their lives. Our culminating event—for which we all worked more than a semester to raise sufficient money—was a formal seven-course dinner at the local grand and historic hotel, featuring toasts, awards, speeches, flowers, and more crystal and silverware than anyone had ever seen on anybody's dining-room table.

For this year, for this class, these students commanded my entire attention. In essence, I did the best for them and with them that I have ever done as a high school teacher. For their part, the students argued, created, wrote, stretched. The level of excellence was, I thought, high, and our discussions were stimulating and broad ranging. It was so ironic, then, that in this class I met a brick wall that I could not negotiate and could not break through.

The wall was Miguel. He was male (one of five in a class of nineteen), African American (one of four in the class). He was intelligent, quiet, mature, the son of a well-known if somewhat feared community activist and single mother. Miguel was a steady and excellent student, and I had had him in class in previous years with no incident. But, as this year went on, it became clear to me that Miguel and I were not clicking.

It started with Miguel's mildly contemptuous air as we discussed the literature we read and, in particular, explored the social implications of that literature. Miguel didn't exactly condescend during those conversations, but he would often decline to talk and, when he did contribute, would make his comments as if he were the only person in the class who knew enough to speak. I assumed that Miguel's background—his mother had fought the white establishment in our small city for many years and had fought it successfully—gave him an earned sense of superiority. At any rate, Miguel withheld himself in most class conversations and even in small groups.

Less engaged is not always that serious, however, and because I had taught Miguel before, I was not alarmed at what I perceived to be a new, if not improved, attitude. But Miguel's stance emerged more clearly during a writing conference when we discussed his draft on *Native Son,* one of our novels and a piece of literature that had inspired whole days of discussion on race and racism. I had questioned the logic of one of his assertions, and he had defended it. Characteristically, Miguel delivered his opinions calmly. But during our conference he told me that I could not respond to his essay on virtually any level and that he could not accept my questions or suggestions. The reason was an unalterable handicap: I was white, and because I was white, I was directly and explicitly culpable, damned, responsible for a number of immoral and heinous events. Because of my race, I was part of the problem and, further, morally unfit to respond to his work. He extended the argument: because of my race I was also not really qualified to be his teacher.

I was not unacquainted with this argument, but I'd never encountered it face-to-face. Certainly at this advanced-placement course's fall opening orientation a number of African American parents had specifically questioned safeguards for justice and balance in this pilot class. Since the school administrators had been aware of these concerns before they had been articulated, the course had been planned so that its content and the makeup of the nineteen students fully reflected the school's—and the community's—diversity. But even at that orientation—when hard questions were asked—no one had said that a white person would be unqualified to teach the course. And later in the year, during class discussions of the writing of James Baldwin,

Richard Wright, and others, we had addressed racial issues. In particular *Native Son* inspired much discussion, and I, on my part, had talked about the implications of growing up in the previously segregated South and, at that time, living in an all-white area of town. Not all of the discussion was easy, but I trusted my students, black and white, and had enjoyed peaceful relations with both racial groups.

But in our writing conference, Miguel's comment gave a new dimension to racial differences. I chewed briefly on Miguel's remarks and then questioned him. As a male, was he individually responsible for the sins of all males, for the rape, for instance, of every woman? I continued: as an American, was he responsible for all the deaths in the not-so-recently-concluded Vietnam War? Miguel did not have answers to these questions, but he was clearly not moved or disturbed. He appeared secure in his assessment, and nothing I could say would change it. I was his white teacher, dismissed, and we ended our writing conference.

Miguel's judgment of me as unfit because of my race proved, for me at least, a barrier to communication. Because I was the only AP English teacher, we were stuck with each other—but, then again, Miguel never asked to leave the class. He simply, I think, wanted me to know that I was, as a Caucasian, unqualified to make an intelligent judgment on him or his work. For my part, though shocked, even sickened, by what I saw was an unresolvable issue, I continued to try to be his teacher. Day after day I acted as if somehow we could work this out. I called on him, responded to him, tried to believe—tried to make both of us believe—that we could approach some sort of détente.

In the succeeding months of the class, we all, as a group, continued to write and discuss and, by most measures, to be harmonious. Miguel was not an overt confronter in class but simply maintained his reserve and his calm decision not to engage in the life of the class. In his writing, he did well on virtually all assignments, and he received deserved A's, positive comments, and, at the end, did well in the course and in his AP exam. For my part, it really wasn't difficult to praise him, but I do know that I did not challenge Miguel or demand that he heavily revise or rework his writing. There was, I know, a hollowness to my dealings with him, and whatever intellectual challenge I could have offered him I instinctively shrank from.

And then, one day, he asked my opinion of which college he should choose: a famous, historical all-black university or a local, land-grant university located in a rural area. The latter boasted less than one percent African American students and faculty and had a mild reputation as a difficult environment for both women and minorities.

Was this a test or a trick? After our previous discussions, after our relationship in class, I was incredulous that Miguel would ask my white opinion on his future. But I responded. I told him that this was really no dilemma: unless the scholarship money was the issue and the land-grant college significantly outbid the all-black institution, the latter was the clear choice. The product of a woman's college, I knew the positive aspects of such an environment and described them to Miguel. Of course he did choose the all-black institution (and I wrote positive recommendations for both universities), but I never understood the conversation. Considering the context of our relationship, was something else going on that I didn't understand? Did he actually trust my judgment? Or was this to see just how prejudiced the white teacher was? But was he that good an actor?

Certainly Miguel wasn't that good an actor at our final banquet, when he was miffed, and told me so, at the wording of his award. The students had, semianonymously, nominated each other for comic/serious achievements in our class, and Most Talkative, Most Determined, Most Likely to Become Dramatic at Any Moment, and similar titles were some of the awards. Miguel's achievement, Most Militant, though an effort to capture his seriousness and his social commitment, was evidently not correct: he told me at the end of the dinner that he should have been Most Radical, and the disgust with which he left was palpable. Clueless, once again, I—who had okayed all the final award names—had failed to get Miguel's point and had offended.

It was fully a year later when I saw Miguel again. I was with friends at a restaurant, and a number of the former AP students were home from college and also eating dinner. Two in the group walked over to visit and invited me to come to their table and greet the others. I did so with pleasure. Miguel, I saw, was also there, and I hoped to hear how he was doing in college and to chat a bit. But the encounter was not positive and not warm: while I exchanged pleasantries and greeted each of my former students at the table, Miguel was silent. He managed only the faintest of acknowledgments, did not respond to my inquiry, and then averted his face in silence. The other students fell quiet too, and it was clear it was time for me to exit. I made my good-byes and returned to my own table; I knew a snub when I saw one, and I wasn't going to press the point or wait around for more.

Why is this failure so poignant for me? Perhaps it hurts, even now, because I tried very hard with this group, I took some serious risks with this class and this student, and I know that I grew a great deal. Perhaps, subliminally, I wanted to be rewarded for my effort, acknowledged for my growth; perhaps I expected each and every one of the students to be appreciative of my efforts and to be even somewhat grateful. Looking back, trying to see it from Miguel's point of view, it was, I assume, a difficult year for him. A light-skinned student, was he enacting his version of the Black Power movement of the time and, essentially, trying to be blacker than black? Was he simply mirroring his mother's famed activism? Was he, a senior restless to get on with his life, reacting against high school? Was he resentful of that very visible part of the elite power establishment as embodied by the AP course itself? Was this more personal, a dislike of me, who also happened to be white?

Whatever it was, after our conversation about his essay, the year teaching Miguel was difficult for me. Aware, as ever, that I could not be in total synch with all my students—no longer their age, not living on their particular streets, often not their gender, often not their class, often not their race—I felt a sense of failure.

I suppose I was disqualified from teaching many of my students. The difference is that only one student told me so.

And the great difficulty is that no amount of effort or skill or even good will on my part could overcome that fact.

Years have passed, and the moral of this story is no moral at all. I take, to this day, Miguel's objections on his own terms: I was white, Miguel was black, and, for him—and perhaps for many other students—that was an irreconcilable difference. That is the sum of the story. It was an insurmountable barrier for Miguel, and because he judged it so, it became impossible for me also. I was a white teacher, and he was a native son. We looked at each other across a great divide, and our relationship withered in the harsh reality of racial differences.

Reference

Wright, Richard. 1957. *Native Son*. New York: HarperCollins.

Culturally Relevant

ELIZABETH CHISERI-STRATER

It's 1970 and I am living in rural Maine. I feel politically hip about my four years of teaching middle school in Bedford Stuyvesant in New York City, where everything I did, I learned from my students. I taught Langston Hughes and Richard Wright. I had students write poetry to jazz and blues music. I visited students' homes and talked with their parents about the importance of books and magazines, I volunteered at the community center on weekends, stayed after school for extracurricular activities, and directed a lively production of Romeo and Juliet that demonstrated the sword-fighting skills of my cast.

I am lukewarm about the position I've taken in this country middle school in Maine but am assured by my success in New York that I'll have much to offer these students. I do a little clean-up work first. When I discover a student sitting in my class holding her book upside down, I inquire about her placement. Oh, don't worry, I'm told. That's a Furbish. She can't read but she won't give you any trouble. Nonsense, I protest: she can be trained to do something useful. I have her tested and shipped off to the local training school along with Harry, the boy whose face was scarred by an unfortunate explosion at the town dump. Home visits begin on the country backroads. Sandy Turcotte offers me a free dog, and when I arrive at her house I meet her fifteen-year-old pregnant sister who has dropped out of school. The following day the teachers share with me that Sandy's father has impregnated all his daughters. It's just a matter of time, they say. I give Sandy my copy of *Our Bodies, Our Selves.* When I'm approached by some students to be the cheerleading coach, I tell the girls that I don't do cheerleading, that I don't believe in women supporting men's teams. I am unable to interpret their quizzical looks.

After Christmas and a quick-march through *The Call of the Wild* because we have a class set, I decide it's time that these students learn about the "underprivileged." With my own money I purchase thirty copies of a novel that my former middle school students loved reading, *Black Like Me*. This nonfiction book by John Howard Griffith is the story of a white man who changes the color of his skin in order to experience what it's like to be black. It depicts his encounters with discrimination in the South as well as his many sexual explorations, sections of the book I had forgotten about.

Parental protest begins fairly swiftly in all my classes. They arrange for visits with me at school to point out the sexually explicit passages, the complex level of the vocabulary, and the inappropriateness of the theme. Smugly, I think, well at least the parents are reading it. Some students are assigned alternative books to read in the library during class time; others are allowed to sit in class and hear the discussions but not to read the book. After all the hoopla, I am positive that students will want to read any book that's been forbidden. Each day that I start my meticulously designed lessons, which include the history of slavery and civil rights, students stare at me disinterestedly. Vocabulary's too hard, I think, and spend hours presenting background words. Again, students resist, complaining that they have farm chores and baby-sitting to do after school. Nonsense, I say, and hand out lots of failing grades. I plug away, sure now that the real problem is peer pressure, that students are afraid to talk about the book. Essay writing will allow them the privacy to reveal their empathy for this man's social bravery. No essays flow in. I stick with the book to the very end of my unit. After it is clear that we are finally done with it, one brave student raises his hand and asks, "Can we read another novel about animals?"

By the end of the year the Furbish girl is back in my class with her book upside down and Sandy is pregnant. Harry's older brother has been sentenced to jail for killing their stepfather. I've been invited to local church services and suppers but I never find time to go. Several cheerleaders have stayed after school to discuss their parents' alcoholism or divorces. But my mind is on the following year, wondering what book I can teach that will help these students understand those less fortunate than them.

References

Boston Women's Health Collective. 1979. *Our Bodies, Our Selves: A Book By and About Women*. New York: Simon & Schuster.

London, Jack. 1977. *The Call of the Wild*. Franklin Center, PA: Franklin Library.

An Embarrassing and Humbling Mistake

GLENNELLEN PACE

I t was 7:45 on a morning in early November 1969. My sixth-grade class of some thirty-six students and I were about to go on our first field trip. We had arranged with parents to gather early, since we'd need more than the normal school day for this adventure.

I was teaching at Freedom Elementary School, located about one-third of the way around the Monterey Bay between Santa Cruz and Monterey. Freedom, California, near Watsonville, is part of the Pajaro Valley School District in an area known as the artichoke capital of the world. At that time, Freedom's students came from rural families, from one recent suburban-type housing development, and from the migrant farm worker population that lived there in the fall and again in the spring.

Family circumstances had suddenly plucked me from Eugene, Oregon, where I was to begin my teaching career, and landed me in Santa Cruz one month before the school year began. I was fortunate, however, to be hired almost immediately for the position in Freedom. I set about getting to know my new surroundings before the school year began. One resource that especially appealed to me was a state-run area near Monterey, overlooking the ocean, where a biologist would guide school groups in studying tide-pool and other near-shore plant and wildlife. I felt eager to return to this place with my very first class of students.

This first year of teaching challenged me from the very first morning of day one when Joey arrived at the classroom door carrying a soft-furred, chocolate-colored rodent with large, deep brown eyes. He announced he was keeping it. (Joey, I found out later, was a troubled boy who had recently witnessed his father kill his mother. He really needed something to care for.) I pulled out all the stops to quickly secure a cage, meanwhile worrying about getting an entire class off to a good start. During lunch I called a biology teacher at the high school to ask what the creature might be and what to feed it. He invited me to bring Joey and the rodent to him that afternoon so he could advise us properly, which we did. It was a vole, we learned; Joey gave serious attention to how to care for it.

The vole became a permanent resident in our classroom. Its appearance on that first day sparked interest and discussion about animals and area wildlife and I thought was a reasonable lead-in to the tide-pool field trip I wanted to arrange. I wanted the trip to happen early in the year; I was struggling to create a successful learning community for this large and diverse group of children and me. I thought a daylong shared experience might create new and important bonds.

So I told my students about the well-populated, colorful tide pools and the sheer cliffs dropping into the sea; none of them had been there. I told the principal about my idea. He approved. The secretary helped me with permission slips. I wrote a letter to parents. My students and I prepared for the upcoming trip. Everyone would have to come to school early on that day to return on time in the afternoon. Together we generated a lot of excitement. This was a very special event for these children.

It was not easy to arrange for all students to manage the extended day—particularly the rural and migrant children. But somehow we made it work. Now the day had arrived, and so had all the students, early, at school, carrying lunches and jackets and itching to go.

But where was the bus? We were to *leave* at 7:45. The bus hadn't even arrived yet, and it was quickly approaching 8:00. I left the class (with strict instructions about behavior—teachers in adjoining classrooms weren't there yet) and ran to the office. The secretary was just arriving. Nearly out of breath, I rushed toward her, telling her the bus hadn't yet arrived, asking her who to call, what to do.

She turned to me, an odd expression washing over her face. "Did you *order* a bus?" she asked.

The breath I had left in my lungs turned to lead and hit the bottom of my stomach. My eyes opened wide. "Was *I* supposed to order the bus?" I gasped. My brief stint at student teaching hadn't included a field trip. I had assumed the papers I filled out for the trip went to someone who then ordered the bus. I felt stupid, and wondered how I'd ever face my students with the news.

I was on the phone immediately, hoping a bus might be available. No luck. The best they could do was take us someplace around 9:30 and return us to the school by 2:00. I asked the secretary to call our biologist guide to cancel and headed to the classroom to face my kids.

I quickly hatched an alternative plan. About seven miles from the school was a large lake and surrounding park. We could go there between 9:30 and 2:00. At the very least I could organize some plant and insect viewing, and we'd play some games and enjoy our lunches. The students chose this option, though I remained chagrined.

I was able to reschedule the original trip sometime later in the year. But this humbling incident to this day reminds me of how easy it is for just about anyone, even when they've tried hard to do everything right, to make what to "those who know" is a "stupid" mistake.

Scenes from the Inner Life of a Teacher

GLENDA L. BISSEX

A
s an adolescent I came to realize that other people had inner lives. I don't remember when in my teaching years I considered the inner lives of other teachers, especially those I looked up to. Perhaps I hesitated to grant them inner lives that would make them merely human, like me, and so change our relationship. Now, in my work with teacher-researchers, I'm privileged to glimpse some of their inner dialog, conflicts, questions, and responses to joyful and painful surprises. Do they know that as a teacher I, like them, have an inner life that is not just intellectual and that has its dark side?

Reading a study by a young teacher-researcher who sometimes reminds me of myself in my early years of high school teaching, I'm startled to realize how different her inner view, as she portrays it, is from my inner view, as I recall it. She sees her problems with an unmotivated class as solvable within weeks or months. I watch her search for readings that will resonate with these young people's lives. I listen to her reasoning about the kinds of assignments that will elicit response. I hear her faith, not only in her students but in herself. Though I, too, reshaped curriculum and generated new teaching strategies as I learned from each day's teaching experiences, I wondered if these weren't Band-Aids on bleeding wounds. The wounds were my character faults. A stronger person wouldn't have backed away from Peter's threat about his grade. A more dynamic person could have fired up today's dragging discussion. A more efficient person would have returned these papers long ago. Who was I to be a teacher? I looked around my school and saw effective, self-confident, established teachers, and I felt alone.

Problems are solvable and mistakes are correctable, while character faults are pervasive and persistent. If my difficulties were largely internal, how could I ask other teachers for help? Asking for help would only publicize the difficulties I shouldn't be having. My constant resolve to improve both my teaching and my character involved a good deal of beating up on myself. I don't know how many other teachers struggle or struggled with this view of themselves because it wasn't something discussed at faculty meetings or even in private conversations with my colleagues.

Teachers are supposed to be in control. Every August I had nightmares of classrooms out of control—nightmares that pursued me long after I had learned a great deal about "managing" my classroom. This is one dream:

> *I am filling an unexpected teaching vacancy at a new version of one of the high schools where I actually taught. I come in in the middle of the day, and since the English department chair is at a meeting, I go right to the classroom without knowing my schedule or anything about the class because it's time to start teaching. I do, however, have a sense that this is an unruly class. As I come into the classroom, I see that the chairman's office and the faculty meeting room are separated from my room only by glass or screening, like a porch, so I'm going to be pretty exposed.*

> *The classroom is divided by a partition that extends lengthwise from the back of the room to within several feet of the front. From my position slightly to one side of this partition, half of the class is not visible yet I feel confident that I will keep things under control. I speak firmly and assuredly to the students on the side of the room I can see, and they respond well. They are all girls, and after class many of them gather around me to talk. I know I have been successful with them—that they like me and want me to teach them.*

> *While I am teaching them, however, I decide to check out what's going on in the half of the classroom hidden by the partition. That's a different story: mostly boys who, though they are silent, are engaged in various pranks. One row has large upholstered cushions on top of them that they pop up from under after I move over to their side of the room. I never actually teach this half of the class, but at least the disruption doesn't spread—in fact it improves when I enter—and they are quiet.*

Who are these unruly students I don't want to see and don't try to teach? They are on the right side of the room—the right side of the brain, the nonlinear, creative side. They are out there in the classroom but they are also within me. They are neither orderly nor obedient. And they are separated off. As a teacher, I have chosen to stand to the left of that partition—in the linear, verbal left side of the brain, which is what schooling is about. Schools can partition off the right side but not eliminate what is beyond conscious control, beyond my determination to manage things and to speak to the students firmly and with assurance. I could interpret my dream as reflecting my partial mastery of control issues yet revealing at the same time what I cannot control and what I thus ignore, allowing it to become more unruly. When I step to the right side of the partition to see what's going on, the subversive, creative energy in my students and in myself is less disruptive.

Successful teaching has its underside whether I see it or not—whether I choose to look at the pranksters on the other side of the partition. Still I proceed, with all the hubris of a teacher—the need to control, the belief in continual learning and in perfectibility—until some angry or unruly student humbles me again. Though I still feel these blows painfully and personally, I'm beginning to understand that my very successes define my limits. I will never be an ideal teacher—dynamic, efficient, knowledgeable, courageous, responsive, always able to listen. I will never be invulnerable. Someone will always be on the other side of that partition, waiting to be seen.

In my case study research course, I devote a lot of attention to the final written report, reading as many drafts as participants show me and responding to each at length. I care about good writing and I see the clarity and focus that revision produces as part of the research process, part of knowing what they've seen. The oral presentations of their research are usually good enough—better than many I hear at conferences—to lull me into neglecting this aspect of the course, except for offering a few guidelines. I feel more confident advising on writing than on public speaking, anyway. Knowing there are some kinds of teaching I do well has finally freed me to acknowledge there are other kinds I'm not so good at. This year I recognized my neglect of the oral work and sought my students' help. Ask your students, I tell my teacher researchers, knowing how much valuable information many have gained when they stopped trying to figure out by themselves what their students thought and asked the students instead. So I asked my students, half hoping somebody would say, But you haven't really neglected this. However, everyone offered suggestions, thus tacitly agreeing there was a problem. One replied, "I appreciate your admission that this part of the course has been neglected—I concur." She wrote a full page of detailed and thoughtful suggestions and argued that learning to make presentations was important. Now that my handling of this part of the course is a matter for public discussion rather than inner anguish, and now that my students' suggestions are openly voiced, I'm committed to making changes.

My inner dialog in response to reading this feedback from participants in my course has not been to brood (more than momentarily) about my character faults but to talk with the new class, sharing some of the previous class's suggestions along with my thoughts and questions about how to guide their future presentations more helpfully. In doing this, I recognize my responsibility as a teacher—my responsibility, in conjunction with my students' responsibility, for the good things that have happened in this course as well as my share of responsibility for its weak spots. I could experience that responsibility as a guilt trip or see in it the opportunity for change, which is how my students saw my question to them.

The underside of teaching is not merely the things that go wrong but the way we view the things that go wrong.

On Kids and Reality Checks

JEROME C. HARSTE

A while back I was invited to do a workshop on whole language in a school in San Bernardino, California. I flew in early to visit several classrooms and thus adjust what I would do and say to make the workshop particularly relevant for these teachers.

The kindergarten teachers knew I had written several children's books and invited me to be a resident author on my visit. When I arrived in the first classroom, the teacher had her class seated in semicircles around a rocker, the place of honor for authors in this room.

Just as I took my place, a second kindergarten class walked in and took its place behind the first; after them a third, and then a fourth. There was a sea of children in front of me. Despite the noise, everyone seemed well mannered, their seats firmly planted on the carpet.

I said hello. They said, "Hello, Dr. Harste!" With little other pomp and circumstance, I began reading *It Didn't Frighten Me!* Immediately Donald, seated in the front row, stood up on his knees. By the time I finished the first set of pages, the admiring sea of children were protesting Donald's behavior, as this meant they couldn't see the pictures. Under duress Donald sat down, but as I read the next set of pages, Donald was up again and so were the protests, more vociferous this time.

Before sitting back down this time, Donald said to me, "I can read that book."

I said, "You can? That's just great!" and continued to read. By the time I finished the next set of pages, Donald was up again—this time standing. "My turn to read," he announced, and grabbed the book out of my hand.

What happened next shocked even me. My whole professional life has been a saga of trying to get books in the hands of children. In the midst of cries of "Don't let Donald read!!!" and "We want Dr. Harste to read!!!" I literally yanked my book out of Donald's hand, the very kind of child for whom I had written the book in the first place!

Thinking fast, I tried to recover. Calling Donald to me, I whispered, "Here, you can have this book to read whenever you want. Oh, look, your teacher would like you to read it to her."

As Donald made his way to the back of the class, I rapidly groped through my duffel bag to find another copy of *It Didn't Frighten Me!* and continued my reading before the class got totally out of hand.

As I continued, I noticed another child. With each succeeding page he got closer and closer to both me and the book. He seemed totally engrossed. By the end of my reading he was literally nose to nose with me and the book. He, too, was standing on his knees by the end of the reading, but this time no one seemed to mind.

I was delighted. I thought, What a great demonstration! Any teacher witnessing this scene knows why I think adults should read to children every day. I need to hire this child and take him with me when I do workshops! What a reader!

To make sure the moment was not lost on the teachers, I thought I would let the child have the first word. Upon finishing, I paused and looked the child right in the eye.

There was dead silence for a moment. The child read my intent well. He was the first to speak. With due concern, he boomed, "Golly, man, what happened to your nose?"

He hadn't been listening to the story at all.

Second Fiddles

MARY BURKE-HENGEN

Welcome to the adult world, a place where weighty ideas are discussed in an open forum, and far away places become familiar."

My room was a stage set inviting the twenty-five sophomores who had signed up for integrated English and global studies to enter and be comfortable, though not too comfortable, in the rigid plastic school chairs placed around heavy tables. Colorful large photo posters of Saudi Arabia, England, Mexico, and Japan hung on the walls, along with pictures, projects, poems, and quotations by former students. I invited this new, lucky group to sit wherever they wished.

I mentally patted myself on the back a lot during the first part of that year. I felt rather clever that I had had the foresight to claim the leavings of a fellow teacher departing for a career in elementary education. His tables and chairs would allow me to set up a perfect rectangle, a seminar kind of arrangement where everyone could see everyone else and, I hoped, listen to everyone else's ideas. Remembering a happy recent experience I'd had in a summer seminar, I thought I might have solved at least one of high school teaching's many mysteries.

At the beginning, it was promising: our conversations were fairly interesting and quite respectful. Understanding that they were asked and expected but not demanded to participate in a mature, thoughtful manner, for a while most students did. What happened as the weeks and months passed, however, was more like my temporarily forgotten, horrific memories of graduate school seminars that didn't work or worked as opportunities for lengthy and competitive jousting more than they did for involvement in learning. A few students saw a wonderful opportunity to shine. And shine they did. By the end of the first semester, they had convinced the rest of the class of their intellectual prowess. Those who loved the limelight practiced skills of intellectual dominance. Slowly, the room became oriented toward who was talking rather than what was said. Unspoken, unacknowledged rules developed that a couple of people could talk as long as they liked without any-one's interjecting. Others, like second fiddle players in a symphony, could make brief comments but were not expected to deliver a sustained solo performance.

Some students responded by tuning out and starting side conversations with each other while I chafed in the role I'd set for myself as seminar leader and participant but not controller. Although I didn't like the patterns of dominance and withdrawal I saw, I believed that in time, students would claim their individual powers. I worked and reworked, trying to fix my hopes. I suggested time limits for individual participation, scoring guides on partici-pation, not-too-subtle recording in the grade book during discussions, side appeals to the kindly to be sure to ask so-and-so questions or to paraphrase rather than judge his comments in order to encourage him. I varied discus-sion with field trips and community service projects at the nearby grade school and the prison; we worked on art projects in small groups and broke into small groups for research and presentations, but the class never became the community of learners I'd envisioned.

My hopes died a hard, hard death. Perhaps it's the chemistry of these individuals, the leadership of a few negative voices; perhaps the materials or the activities aren't quite right; and worst of all, perhaps I am getting too old to teach adolescents, I thought. At the end of the year, I interviewed several students on audiotape about the class and played and replayed the tapes over the summer. Their responses varied from "In this class, I was challenged, and it was a good experience" to "I was afraid to say much." It bothered me very much that some students felt silenced by others, the opposite of my inten-tions for the seminar, and I made significant changes in the curriculum and activities for the class. I returned the next fall in anticipation of a better year. By November, I understood it wasn't going to be a better year, and after a particularly frustrating day when students had not only not listened but had shown a general disregard for one another and for the ideas being put forth, I decided it was time we stopped and talked about the class before we limped further into disarray.

I don't know what it was that night after school as I stood in the center of the room that told me to push the tables back and put all the chairs in the middle of the room in a circle. Perhaps it was a subliminal message from a lesson a counseling intern had taught the students about circles and their meaning in Native American life or some refound wisdom born of experi-mentation with physical settings and how they affect learning over three-plus decades of teaching that finally overcame the blinders I was wearing. When the students came in the next day and sat down, there was a dramatic and desirable difference in their behavior. They shared many more of their thoughts and feelings and listened to one another in the way I had imagined the seminar arrangement would encourage them to do. In the days that followed, I began to reenjoy my teaching. I reflected anew on the powers of proximity and access to one another that any school community needs to flourish.

After a couple of months of the new arrangement, however, many students came in complaining about the same old circle. "The circle again?" "Are we going to do this every day?" "I can't work when we sit here." "Have you been to some conference about this?" By this time, I was painfully aware of how rigid my thinking had been about the first room arrangement, and I felt deep regret over letting my desire for a plan to work keep me from seeing how well the plan actually did work for my students. I was willing to make whatever changes would result in a classroom environment that encouraged all students to do well in the class. I negotiated with them to keep the circle arrangement as our basic conversation and discussion tool but to vary it from day to day so that two days a week would be independent reading and writing with independent seating arrangements, another day a week would be spent in small-group projects and arrangements, and two days would start with circle discussions and oral readings. Sometimes I moved the tables into isolated units, and sometimes I pushed them all into the middle of the room, opening up the peripheral spaces in front of the bookshelves and windows. The tables became enjoyable flat surfaces for mural painting and other construction projects.

I rediscovered that there are many, many physical arrangements to be used with any class, depending on purpose. By committing to one method, I was trapped in a magnification of the downside or failings of that method. Unfortunately, the students were stuck there with me, and they weren't any more aware at the time than I was of why our group wasn't forming into a supportive learning community.

I also discovered anew how central building community is to effective and joyful teaching and learning. If a class is not a place where respect, belonging, and support are consistently present, it becomes as dreary and destructive as the factory job I once had where only the women with seniority could move the fans that cooled our hot faces. As I sweltered through 90- to 100-degree heat that summer, I grew resentful of my powerless position and became a less kind and gentle person with every passing day. It doesn't matter how fine our educational goals might be: they often do not penetrate through what students experience as a mean-spirited atmosphere.

Nor are students likely to ask questions in a situation where they cannot trust how those questions will be treated. Setting up what seemed to me an egalitarian classroom did not mean that students acted in their own or one another's best interests. Sophomores are, after all, sophomores. They cannot be expected to be aware of one another in the way a teacher needs to be aware of her students, nor can they be expected to possess much wisdom about the long-term results of their behavior. In my desire for democratic spirit, I created a kind of oligarchic monster. This has led me to question the meaning I have held for the term *student-centered* and what the term implies about day-to-day realities of interaction and learning. I think now that although it means that I listen and observe students and am open to their diverse ways of expressing similar goals, it also means that I protect the rights of all students: no student should ever feel like a second fiddle. Not much can be learned in an atmosphere of threat of intimidation from peers. Although I learn many things in the company of my students, I cannot dwell for long in an equal relationship. I need to exercise definitive leadership toward larger community/collaborative learning-centered goals.

Although I tell my students that acknowledging and accepting mistakes is a vital part of the learning process, I don't easily apply this to myself. More than anything, I regret my sureness that I was right about the seminar plan and room arrangement. I am tentative about so many things in my teaching, and yet I wasn't suspicious of the method even when early signs told me something wasn't working. I know I told myself that what I was doing was different from what students were accustomed to and so it would need time. I was so tenacious about it, something else I try to teach the students, but it was not the time for tenacity; I needed flexibility and responsiveness.

In retrospect, I think that in part I missed many clues to what was and wasn't happening in my seminar classroom because I was so unsure of myself as a high school teacher. It had been over twenty years since I had taught this age group, and the return was one of the most difficult parts of my teaching career. I was struggling with many aspects of teaching as much as I had when as a beginner I threw up my breakfast before entering the classroom. I know that I didn't yet have a renewed sense of adolescent behavior, and little of my teaching knowledge was able to be intuitive. Feeling insecure, I adopted a false sense of surety. I feel bad about my mistake, most especially the length of time I stayed with the seminar arrangement, yet I am glad that I did learn what I needed to learn in order to become a better teacher for my students.

Y'All Chill, Mrs. K.

MARY MERCER KROGNESS

I can still hear fifteen-year-old seventh-grader Jawan's admonition: "Y'all chill, Mrs. K." Such succinct and sound advice, and spoken to me so comfortingly. I didn't exactly chill, but I weathered eighth grader Lisa's outlandish behavior, particularly the morning she waltzed into our language arts class wearing a form-fitting T-shirt with large, grotesque plastic hands placed strategically and the words I HAVE A HOLD OF MYSELF emblazoned across her chest. The boys' eyes were out on stems; this class period was already off to a sorry start. Eventually I regrouped.

On another day a boy and a girl in my most talented and usually most productive class of low and underachieving seventh and eighth graders were out of their seats and swinging. Katreece, taller than Malik, quickly gained the advantage with a hammerlock. I was stunned by their incendiary fight. I jumped between them while they yelled at and hit each other and called for my other students to telephone the office and to try to restrain the combatants. Before the order was out of my mouth, the kids responded with unusual speed and calm. The blowup, over a comment by Katreece to Malik about his personal hygiene, stopped as suddenly as it had erupted. Without exception my students demonstrated maturity and kindness. I learned not to stand between kids doing battle.

I also managed to keep my cool when Carrie brazenly yelled, "Bitch," because I'd asked her to take her seat. I tried not to look jarred when smart but impulsive Jess filled a condom with water and popped it into a congested corridor just a few seconds prior to his coming to my class. I even kept a level head when I got wind that one of my boys was harboring a loaded gun in his locker. My point in telling these war stories (we *all* can tell them) is to say that I survived; often I learned from these brushes with classroom chaos.

But a challenge that positively unnerved me and eventually wearied my spirit was a class of the most silent—and it turned out the most passive—eighth graders I'd ever encountered. (Everyone who's taught eighth graders knows that as a rule they are anything but passive. And if they are, there's a problem.) On the first day of school, this particular group sat quietly—almost motionless—and stared, waiting, I suppose, for me to tell them what to do. In my eagerness to waste not a minute in engaging them, I set about preparing the young people to do a brief (and I imagined unthreatening) exercise in which they would pair up and introduce their classmates and me. First we generated a meager bank of questions they could rely on during their interviews. Instead of asking each other questions, mostly they sat and looked at each other. And when it came time for the pairs to make introductions, they alternately mumbled a few words about people's favorite foods and colors or some other Trivial Pursuit information or they cracked jokes and jived each other, then sat down and waited.

Feeling slightly bewildered, I asked: "So, what have you learned about each other?"

"Nothin' that we don't already know," a girl snapped.

"You know *everything* about each other?" I asked.

One boy smirked, "I know as much as I wanna know—especially about . . ." and he named the two boys and three girls who could least afford to be ridiculed by a peer, by anyone for that matter. Those five kids squirmed uncomfortably amid snickers.

Considering that most of my students traveled together from the time they got on the school bus in the morning until they rode home late in the afternoon, and noting that the majority of these kids were placed in basic-track classes together, their not wanting to know one another better or become engaged in learning should not have come as a surprise. These particular kids were required to take language arts/reading, the class I taught, because they scored at or below the third stanine in reading comprehension and vocabulary on the Stanford Achievement Test. Most of them had been placed in the basic-track English, math, and science classes and, during seventh grade, the lowest level of social studies too. I was seeing the full effect of the unsavory practice of tracking or leveling students (and poor pedagogy, according to hundreds of research studies in which the harms of tracking students are documented); I was witnessing the liabilities of an old and convenient school practice that is also politically loaded.

The system of tracking or leveling students, particularly common at the secondary level, breeds a peculiar kind of incest. As I watched this silent, brooding bunch of eighth graders—teenagers who varied in age from the usual thirteen- or fourteen-year-olds up to sixteen—I imagined how little opportunity they'd had in school to observe peers who behaved in ways other than acting out or being utterly passive. Because they'd been tracked, my students had had almost no experience in being with a variety of young people their age who had learned to initiate conversation and raise questions in class, to enjoy and understand curriculums from a different vantage point, and to experience school and even their teachers differently. I also observed my students, who often moved en masse from class to class, feeding off one another's weaknesses rather than being nourished and inspired by their classmates' intellectual, creative, social, emotional strengths. The truth? Frequently, low expectations and uninspired, routine, or inappropriate curriculums had been the rule for the low- and underachieving students; programmed learning kits, skills sheets, and what I call connect-the-dots exercises often constituted the fare for students assigned to the lowest track.

I won't forget the day big Jawan (who'd advised me to chill) made a startling comment. In preparation for reading Mildred Taylor's rich novel *Roll of Thunder, Hear My Cry,* what I consider the most important young adult novel available to young people, my seventh graders and I were in the throes of discussing the separate but equal schools in the South and the hand-me-down textbooks given to Cassie Logan and her siblings, star characters in the story.

"Hey, Mrs. K., is *this* a slow class?" When I pressed Jawan to say more about our language arts/reading class—to explain why he thought this class was a skills class—he looked around the classroom and said, "Well look who's in here!" Curious, the rest of the kids didn't seem to be insulted by Jawan's insinuation that everyone (except for him) was a low- or underachieving student. But they did respond to his observation of ours being a class of basic-skills students. Eventually the rest of the young people conveyed their sadness at being slotted and slighted and thought of by their teachers as the least capable kids in our school. Jawan's question, "Is this a slow class?" was, of course, at the heart of the self-esteem issue that we educators often pay lip service to but in our daily practice don't really connect with the act of learning and the promise that all can students become successful learners. Even those of us who intellectually understand the powerful connection between a student with a healthy self-concept and the freedom that confident young person feels to actively engage in learning haven't really grasped the potent impact of the tracking system on students' self-esteem. By agreeing to teach in a school district that tracks its students, we tacitly agree to perpetuate a system that does indeed level their self-esteem, their dreams for the future, and the regard they have for themselves, their classmates, and even their teachers. (Not surprising, teachers who teach basic-skills classes are often thought less able by students, colleagues, and parents—especially in comparison with those who teach the advanced classes.)

The juxtaposition of Jawan's question about ours being a class established especially for less able kids with the earlier conversation that he, his classmates, and I had been having about separate but equal schools in the South, the outdated textbooks issued to the black students in the story, and Jim Crow gave me greater insight into Jawan's innate intelligence and his ability to get at the crux of certain gritty human questions and subtly—intuitively—connect the piece of literature we were reading that day in school with societal issues of class and race and, not incidentally, the practice of tracking students in a democracy. After we spent time hashing over our school's practice of tracking students according to Stanford Achievement Test scores and expressing indignation about students' being labeled and trapped and dismissed by other teachers and students, I led us back to the text of Taylor's remarkable novel and read aloud this excerpt in which Miss Crocker has just issued her pupils badly soiled, worn, outdated textbooks:

> *[Little Man's] brows furrowed. Then his eyes grew wide, and suddenly he sucked in his breath and sprang from his chair like a wounded animal, flinging the book onto the floor and stomping madly upon it. . . . He just stood staring down at the open book, shivering with indignant anger. (p. 17)*

My students, who had sat in rapt attention while I read, jumped to their feet and cheered. I marveled at their strength and resilience, but on this day I more fully understood the effects of the tracking system on young people and vowed to join like-minded teachers and parents to derail and ultimately dismantle it.

Reference

Taylor, Mildred. 1976. *Roll of Thunder, Hear My Cry.* New York: Dial.

The Essential Web

MEG PETERSEN

Something was wrong—something more than a normal first-day awkwardness. As I explained the syllabus and course requirements we would follow in Introduction to Literature, I felt the pace of my speech increasing. The words raced on as if to fill some indefinable void. I closed off every statement with a feeble tag question—you know? you see? No one seemed to. I could read nothing in their faces. I threw out lines, hoping for response, for connection. It was eerie; I could hear myself breathing, hear the chalk scraping on the board as I wrote my name.

I then had students respond in writing to questions designed to explore their feelings about reading and literature. It seemed sensible. I thought the exercise would lead to discussion. As they wrote in utter silence, I ran my unseeing eyes over the syllabus. Something within me froze. For the first of many times with this class, my courage failed. I collected their papers and let them go early. In the whole class period, I had been the only one to utter more than a one-word response.

This beginning was chilling, but I was stubbornly hopeful. I assumed they had had bad experiences in literature classes before. My first set of assigned readings, Whitman's "A Noiseless Patient Spider" and Ashbery's "Paradoxes and Oxymorons," were designed to establish the tone of the class. Students would instantly connect, I assumed, with my intended message of acceptance of divergent responses to text. They would be relieved that I wasn't demanding one correct interpretation. This would free them to open up and to draw lines of connection between literature and life. I felt confident in my ability as a teacher to relate to each of them and to help each of them relate to the material. I walked into class my second day and invited them to respond to the poems. They stared uneasily at each other in silence for a long moment.

Finally, Adrienne raised her hand. "Well, I think it means," she began, "that the author is suggesting a relationship between the spider and his soul.

Both are making connections, combating their feelings of isolation by spinning a web for themselves. It's kind of like us making connections with these poems."

After another few moments of silence in which I tried to recover from her having already said everything I wanted the discussion to bring out about the poem, I asked, "What do the rest of you think?"

Not a single pair of eyes met mine. The only sound was the rustling of papers and sneakers on the carpeted floor. This scene would become dreadfully familiar in the weeks to come. Adrienne, slightly older than the others, but still in her early twenties, could easily have made a career out of literary criticism. When I would ask, "What did you think of the story?" she would respond with a carefully thought out, sophisticated interpretation. As most of the class hadn't yet figured out the details of the plot, she intimidated them, albeit unintentionally.

A horrifying (at least for me) pattern had been established in which I would throw out a general question, hoping for a free exchange of ideas. Adrienne would respond, although increasingly grudgingly. She told me she liked to talk in class but didn't like to be the only one to talk. I could certainly understand the feeling.

After her response and the silence that would inevitably meet it, things would degenerate to where I appeared to be playing some bizarre game of twenty questions with the class. "Did you like the story?" I would ask. They soon learned not to answer even this as I would pounce upon them with "Why?" to which they would most likely respond, "I don't know." Then I would be reduced to repeating, "You just didn't like it, huh?"

I tend to be optimistic about things, but I had to admit the class was not going well. I hate to lecture, yet my attempts to generate discussion were utter failures. Sometimes I would talk just to fill the silence—not lecture exactly, more like empty chatter loosely related to the text. I tried every technique I had heard about or read about, even some I devised myself. Nothing penetrated the thick fog through which we operated. In-class freewrites were completed without enthusiasm. Students would stop writing long before the allotted time limit and would read what they had written only when I directly asked them to. I dreaded walking into the stifling atmosphere of the room. Seating students in a circle did nothing to improve the situation. We only sat in a circle, silently avoiding one another's eyes.

The few men in the class had begun to congregate at the back of the room, leaning their chairs against the windows and regarding me with expressions painfully close to sneers. One was helpful enough to inform me that sitting in a circle wasn't working but declined to offer any alternative suggestions. He seemed to take a certain pride in his inability to learn—a pride he and his friends nurtured in the long weeks that followed.

Their first assigned papers seemed to nail the coffin shut. As students were unwilling to discuss the literary works and I didn't provide lectures, confusion about the material was never cleared up. They also lacked experience with writing. Most had been placed in this course because there were no open slots in composition classes. In short, their first papers were a horror. The poor grades they were receiving confirmed their feelings about their lack of ability to understand literature. They assumed I had finally awakened to what they had known all along.

The boys at the back of the room had given up. Unfortunately, they continued to attend class. Although they weren't openly defiant, they rolled their eyes or shifted them away from mine and seemed to be subtly mocking my efforts to engage them in discussion.

By midterm, I was walking into the class at the last possible minute, taking my time. I came to know the clock well. I shuffled papers around on my desk, trying to ignore the daily sensation of drowning.

I survived by relying heavily on two techniques. One was Langer's written conversation. Students were paired up and wrote back and forth, asking and answering questions about the literature. Reading these conversations confirmed what I had in my wildest moments begun to doubt. There were minds out there. They could work through their ideas and explore their confusion, even connect literature to their lives, when they didn't have to risk doing it publicly. But I couldn't have them spend the rest of the semester seated in silence, passing notes back and forth. And when I tried to bring some of this thinking out in front of the class, it no longer appeared to exist.

I fell to placing them in groups to work on questions about the poems and stories. Honestly, it was more an admission of defeat than a teaching strategy. Although it would have been devastating to my self-esteem to have admitted it, I was giving them the equivalent of worksheets to avoid having to look into their unresponsive and sometimes hostile faces for interminable fifty-minute blocks.

Some groups worked quite well, others drifted on and off of the task. Some had lively discussions but wrote very little. Others assigned most of the work to one member of the group and relied on that person to supply the answers. This was better than staring at one another in silence, but not much.

Meanwhile, I was thankful that my composition class was going tolerably well. I felt more involved with those students because of their writing and our weekly conferences. I had little idea of what was going on in my literature students' heads. By midsemester, I had barely learned all their names. Perhaps personal contact was the missing ingredient. I asked them each to meet with me for a short conference outside of class. I told them quite frankly I was not happy in the class, didn't think they were either, and wanted their help to make the situation better.

The students who seemed most negative about the class did not show up for their conference. I was struck by how little those who did come in expected out of their education. Most said the class was going fine, better than some of their other classes, and they were most concerned about their grades. The majority said they "just didn't talk in class anyway" and never had. It didn't have anything to do with my class in particular. The interviews seemed to be leading me nowhere. Only when I talked with Kristin did I begin to get a hint of what was going on.

Kristin's group, comprised entirely of women who rarely contributed to class discussions, was usually the quickest to finish the question exercises, settling for the fewest words to answer the questions in the narrowest sense. Because they often finished so rapidly, I would return their paper to them, prodding them to extend their responses. They would add the minimum necessary to satisfy me. When they finished, they would sit in silence, reading the next selection in their anthology.

Kristin complained that sometimes the people in her group didn't do the work, hadn't read the story, or let others find the answers to the questions. This made her so mad she wanted to do the same thing to get back at them. After a pause, she shyly suggested that maybe some ice-breaking exercises at the beginning of the semester would have helped students feel comfortable talking with each other.

Melissa completed the ideas Kristin had hinted at. Melissa was one of two juniors in a class of first-semester freshmen. She was an elementary education major, brimming over with enthusiasm about teaching and eager to help me with my problem. She said she enjoyed the readings. Unlike all of the others, she said she liked to talk in her classes and loved to get into discussions.

This was the moment I had been waiting for. "Then why don't you talk in mine?"

"Oh," she said, "Because Blake and those guys in the back—you know the guy who comes in with his head shaved and the Iron Maiden T-shirt and that other guy, Tom, who always acts so bored with everything?"

I nodded.

"Well, they look at me like I've got three heads every time I open my mouth in that class—God, they even look at *you* like *you've* got three heads when you ask a question. They make fun of that girl Sasha every time she says something. I mean, it takes a lot of courage to get past that. And then there are those two girls—I don't even know their names—who come in late all the time and pass notes about their boyfriends—I mean really! I think I was more mature than that when I was a freshman. I just shut up so I don't have to put up with the way they look at me every time I speak!"

Bingo. She had named the elusive something I'd been trying to put my finger on all semester. The network of relationships in the classroom destroyed any possibility of the type of atmosphere of open discussion I was trying to create. The community was dysfunctional.

I started to consider things about the class I hadn't paid much attention to before. Out of a class of thirty students, twenty-seven were first-semester freshmen and twenty-four were women. The six men in the class huddled together at the back of the room. Five of them worked together in the group question exercises. While they never actually refused to do anything I asked of them, they did radiate negativity in a thousand subtle ways. I had felt the pressure Melissa described as "feeling like I had three heads." I had viewed this as a problem in my relationships with those few students. Through ignoring and refusing to acknowledge their effects on the others, I had given the class over by default to the boys in the back. Emotionally, they were in control.

Negative community poisons subtly. No great overt thing was eating away at the fabric of classroom life, but a thousand small acts of omission and commission drained everyone's energy minute to minute and robbed the experience of any possibility of joy.

Melissa's revelation came too late to salvage that particular class. It took several semesters to gain enough distance from the experience to be able to use what I learned from it.

While I believed in having students work together, believed in collaboration, I had ignored the web of relationships in my classroom. I had ignored the quality of those relationships and failed to nurture and shape them or build an atmosphere in which ideas could flourish.

We enter a classroom at the appointed time, on the appointed day, as teacher and students randomly joined by choice, chance, convenience, or computer program. From that moment, we create our shared history. We begin throwing out lines of contact, of interrelationship, creating the structure of the web of relatedness that will both support and constrain everything that follows.

As teachers, we often accept what we are given. Some classes are better than others. We seem to think community shouldn't matter, and in any case, not much can be done about it. Suppression is the best answer. Eliminate student interchanges as much as possible.

I had always thought about my teaching in terms of relationships with students. But my focus was always on *my* relationship with *individual* students. I made an effort to establish communication and to reach each one of them. But I had ignored the overall community—the quality of students' connections to one another. Of course, for however much of a presence I am in my classroom, I cannot totally control the way relationships will form there. But neither can I afford to ignore those relationships.

I had done nothing to nurture a climate in which ideas, especially the tentative, emerging ones that characterize our responses to literature, could find acceptance. I had expected that only my invitation was necessary to ignite lively discussion. I sat prepared to respond to ideas that were never put forth. This left a void that the elements in the class best acquainted with failure rushed in to fill.

The web of classroom relationships is always there, no less real for its elusive and variable nature. It defines how we will feel when we walk into that classroom. These relationships are not peripheral to learning to make sense of literature or to learning anything else. I now pay attention to them, draw attention to them, and work to shape them.

Skating Under the Ice

JUDITH FUEYO

'm a planner when it comes to my teaching. Generally, I plan class sessions to include three related chunks, each different in time and rhythms. For example, I plan to lecture/write during one part, to invite students to talk/write for another, and to engage us all in a not necessarily verbal experience for another. Once I have this shape figured out, the feeling before class begins builds for me, not unlike those feelings I get before making an entrance onstage in a community theater production. To get up for class, I need the "green room," time apart from the hubbub of my world.

Last year my daughter, Jo, lived with me to save dormitory fees at the university. On Wednesday nights, we frequently traveled home together from the university for a quick supper and back—she to the library and me to my class. It took her several weeks into our first semester to get it—that I wasn't "dissing" her but simply going inward that hour or so before I teach. It's my habit after all these years. I never gave it a name before, but it is as vital to my preparation as any transparencies or lecture notes.

But twice in my teaching career, I could do no more than show up, forget get up, for my teaching. Both times, life so knocked me for a loop that it was all I could do to get up each morning. The first time, I taught seniors in high school; the second time, I taught undergraduates and graduate students at the university. During those times, which lasted from several long weeks to nearly a year, I learned that teaching and learning are not necessarily what I believed, that letting go might be more powerful than planning.

That first time life interfered with my teaching I had taken over a job teaching high school seniors for a woman who quit midyear, giving no notice other than, "They are animals. Good luck, fools." During my interview, the principal said, "You don't want this job. The kids are out of control." Well, I needed the job, so I recited something brave or foolhardy and got it.

The first day of class, one young man walked into the classroom on top of the desks. On a day in spring another young man dropped the diction-

106

ary—as big as the clichéd breadbox—out the window down the three floors to the pavement, past the principal's office below us. Another day, someone left me with a sickeningly wet glob of chewin' tobacca on the rear wall. And during finals, one young woman dropped a lighted match into the wastebasket. Needless to say, I wasn't the best disciplinarian—nor the best teacher. (Interesting how these two are related!) Mornings I'd arrive early to get in line at the copy machine to ensure "enough work" to get me through the day.

Abruptly, my mornings at the copy machine were consumed instead by early visits to a dying husband's hospital bed. From there I'd rush to school into five preparations, seven classes, one hundred and thirty-two kids expecting me to teach. My memory of those weeks and months is of a little *Julius Caesar,* some grammar and usage worksheets left by the quitter, and lots of stories about my dying husband, my three children, and myself. These stories led to the students' stories, and as you can imagine, we came together in ways more human than I'd managed before. One day, I was in the library piling up resourses for an upcoming unit, and my most notorious student called out, "Yo! Mrs. Fueyo, want some help with that stuff?" A colleague nearby whispered to me, "He never calls anybody Mrs. He only utters four-letter words." His buddy even offered to paint my car for a great price because, "You tell it like it is, Mrs. F." I doubt he passed his *Julius Caesar* unit. Perhaps if I'd acted more on my intuitions and less on the materials, he would have. And recall that fire in the wastebasket after the final? I never reached that girl.

Many years and students later, now at the university, I once again needed to subsist on the stuff of my life. Following a series of moves and losses, one a teenage daughter, I became clinically depressed. Below is a passage from a short story I wrote shortly after that time, to give you a sense of where I was. The story was, of course, poorly disguised autobiography. The main character, Sheila, is adjusting to her empty nest without a houseful of teenagers, without a husband. She remembers how things felt just months before.

Coming home from the university tonight, Sheila pulls into the Shop-N-Save. The solidity of the pavement beneath her feet triggers a sensation of last year. Then, outdoor terrain was transparent glass, fragile, as if she might crash through and roam Houdini-like beneath the glassy ice, viewing others' comings and goings from the underside. Oddly, looking back on that time-out-of-time, living a seismic slice below the cosmetic face of the town felt privileged, even superior: no eyes to meet or avoid, no appointments to keep or cancel, nothing was natural, all was supranatural—above and outside the very concept of natural. Freed from "real expectations" ("Reality is nothing but convention dressed in a three-piece suit." Was it Lily Tomlin, compliments of Jane Wagner, who said that?), Sheila'd wandered a parallel path, semiaware of herself on top, say at the crosswalk at Bullocks and University Drive, and simultaneously aware of other selves. A clarity of vision reserved for the un-sane.

Even though I/Sheila was given time off from work, once I came back I was not ready. But I showed up, skating under the ice. During one particular evening class with graduate students, I was unable to hide my feelings when several asked me how my daughter was doing. I spoke to them for several minutes of our struggles. Then silence . . . and a palpable wave of energy moved toward me from them. On several evenings, I admitted to my students that I was unprepared, that they would have to decide what they needed from me and one another and we'd go from there. That semester, the literacy portfolios those students constructed were unlike any I'd seen before. One student wove pieces of personal correspondence from his male lover into his vision of literacy. Another documented her own literacy transactions surrounding her mother's terminal cancer. Once again, by default, I learned to trust my humanity and to distrust myself when I try to "teach" more than to "be." Once again, I learned to let students lead and, to give them the time and responsibility to do it. Sure, I always preached these platitudes, but rarely did I truly follow through.

Or something like that. No doubt all this remembrance is romanticized in the remembering. I haven't mentioned how I cried the day I plied that wad of tobacco off my secondary classroom wall, or how afraid I was of losing my job once word of the fire incident spread. Yet, the peculiar energy of those difficult days lingers with me still.

I am lucky to be in this liminal world now, to have enormous content freedom; for to teach writing, one must lurch into life. I'm lucky that my roots in education and English excuse lots. That is, if one needs excuses for turning teaching occasions into encounters with life's nitty-gritty. Perhaps that's why I survive in this work: I am allowed to make content of my own and of my students' lived lives. Life is the curriculum.

Weather Wise

JANE DOAN

There! That's a weather station, I thought as I closed the door to our Little Room. Penny, my coteacher, and I had recently decided that the Little Room between our classrooms was an ideal space for dramatic play. During our space theme the children had used it as a space shuttle and had thoroughly enjoyed learning about space through their dramatizing. Now we were beginning our weather theme and I had decided that for the next two months the Little Room would become a "weather station." What could be better than using a professional set of weather instruments to get the children involved in our study of weather? I wondered.

I looked back into the Little Room. The meteorological instruments I had borrowed from the Area Resource Center were quietly registering their data. The anemometer, barometer, hygrometer, and thermometer, which measure, respectively, wind speed, air pressure, humidity, and temperature, all appeared to be in working order. I chuckled as I reflected on my discussion with the custodian about installing the equipment on the roof. Although I had offered to do it myself, he had insisted that teachers are not allowed on the roof. We couldn't be trusted to be careful. The roofing material would get damaged. Roof climbing was definitely his domain as far as he was concerned, and I was happy to agree with him. I knew that I would owe him greatly for this favor, but it was worth it to have authentic scientific equipment collecting our weather data.

My gaze turned to the clipboards with the data collection sheets, all ready for the children to start in on Monday. They would be able to collect the weather station information, check the rain gauge outside our classroom, and prepare a weather report for the class. Books on cloud formations and other natural weather predictors would help the children become weather forecasters if they so chose. As far as I was concerned, everything was ready. I expected the children would have as much fun as meteorologists in the Little Room as they did as astronauts.

"Today we have a new activity for Choice Time," I began first thing Monday morning as I explained to the children how the Little Room had been changed from the space shuttle into a weather station. They could sign up to be meteorologists on the Choice Boards either in Penny's room or mine. The children listened politely and then went off to make their choices. To my surprise, no one selected the "weather station."

"Penny, what can we do?" I wailed on Monday afternoon. I was distressed that the children were not interested in studying the weather. "Give the kids some time," Penny calmly stated. "As we study meteorology they will get more complete background information. They will understand more about what a meteorologist does. Then they will want to be in the weather station."

"Maybe," I said, "but until then, I think we should assign kids to be meteorologists each day. That way everyone will get a turn, and I bet they will love it once they actually spend time in the Little Room using all that real scientific equipment."

"Sure," agreed Penny. "We'll sign the kids up. Once they see how much fun it is, then they will choose the weather station on their own." Somehow, though, I felt that there was something missing in my plan.

One month later, I found myself saying to Penny, "You know, this weather station just has not excited the kids. They are willing to spend time there on their assigned days, but no one is very thrilled about it. It seems that everyone is relieved when the assigned weather watching tasks are over. No one has asked for a second turn."

"Mmmm," Penny concurred. "There must be something we can learn from this. Let's keep observing the kids. Perhaps soon they will develop an interest in the weather station."

Two months later, I confessed to Penny, "Well, I'm not sure what I have learned with this theme. The kids did learn a lot about weather. When the meteorologist from the local TV station visited last Friday, he was surprised at all they knew. But, the learning was mostly facts. There was not much they could use for problem solving or for predicting weather. There was none of the practical learning I had hoped they would get from being meteorologists. The children never did enjoy being in the weather station I set up. They never really wanted to go there at Choice Time. I wonder why?"

Penny and I reflected on how I had determined by myself what the Little Room would become. Then we realized that I had decided what materials and activities would be available to the children there. I had decided to call the Area Resource Center and ask for their materials. I had asked the custodian to set up the weather equipment on the roof. I had made every plan and every decision. "I see my mistake!" I exclaimed as the light bulb went on. "The children had no ownership of the weather station. I owned it all and they just never became interested in my idea."

"We've both learned something," Penny replied. "From now on, whenever we start a new theme we will allow the children to decide for themselves what the Little Room will become. We will give them the time to make the materials necessary to turn the Little Room into whatever they have planned it to be. And the children will be the ones to determine what dramatic play will occur there."

The next Monday at 9:45 A.M., I announced, "We are starting our new theme, growing things, today. Let's spend this Investigations Workshop deciding what the Little Room should become." The ideas flew fast and furiously.

"A garden!" shouted Hannah.

"A backyard! My backyard—lots of stuff grows there," suggested Adam.

"A greenhouse would be great," added Jenny. "My mom owns one and she could help us."

"I know lots of things grow in a rain forest," stated Nathan. "I would like to turn the Little Room into a rain forest."

Within five minutes we had more suggestions than we needed! A quick vote, and the Little Room became a greenhouse. The children decided what activities would take place there. They took over the responsibility of setting up the greenhouse and keeping it well stocked. Every day several children chose to spend our Choice Time working in the greenhouse. Many children were repeat horticulturists. And their learning was as dramatic as their play. The greenhouse was a definite success.

This discovery took place three years ago. Since then the children in our primary multiage class have had the responsibility for planning and developing what takes place in the Little Room. Dramatic play in the Little Room has become a favorite Choice Time activity. The children have shown us that when they can decide what they will do and how they will learn, they become actively involved in that learning.

That children can be and even should be responsible for setting up their own learning environments seems such a simple concept. I'm glad I finally caught on!

Changing the Shape of Teaching: Two Teachers in the Classroom

JOANN PORTALUPI AND PEGGY MURRAY

We met at the Tin Palace, a local restaurant where earlier we had talked about the reading methods course we were preparing to coteach. It was way past the semester now, and the class was over. Between us lay the manila envelope that held our student evaluations. We had agreed to read them together. We knew they'd be tough, but neither of us were expecting the anger we found poured out on the pages:

> [The teachers] seemed to contradict each other too often to be effective in their teaching.

> [This] course should not have been team taught. They were two opposites trying to pretend they had the same beliefs.

> I thought I would love coteaching, I hated it! I felt like these two teachers seemed to have no idea what the other's beliefs were, and they continually disagreed with each other, which made it difficult to have my own stance.

> Grading was never clearly stated or explained. I felt we were left in the dark throughout the semester.

Anyone who has sat with a pile of student evaluations knows that the negative comments tend to erase the positive ones. Certainly we wanted to explain away these comments, to focus on those students for whom the class had worked. Nonetheless, as we sat over coffee we considered: Might there have been deep underlying philosophical differences between us? Had there been tensions we unknowingly transmitted to students? If there had been, we couldn't immediately see it. In preparing the course we had easily agreed on selected readings. We both saw the need for bringing in students' personal histories, challenging their notions of reading, creating a classroom community in which they could experience firsthand the way in which an individual's understanding and awareness is promoted and enhanced through the diversity of perspectives. Still many of the evaluations had been negative.

If an ability to develop good teaching relationships lies at the heart of good teaching, these comments and the fragmented relationships they reveal suggest that for these students our teaching failed. Part of that failure is attributed to the fact that there were two of us. What does coteaching entail in the context of the university classroom? One thing is clear; it amplifies certain problems present in the institutional teaching/learning process: What constitutes real learning? Where does authority lie? How does one manage the dizzying process and fallacies of grading?

What Constitutes Real Learning?

The presence of two teachers posed a challenge to those students who were looking simply to receive knowledge. Our view of learning relied on the multiple voices in the classroom to help students reach deeper understanding. Even the readings we selected mirrored this notion of multiple perspectives—Heath (1982), Freire (1991), Rosenblatt (1991). Some students expected us to act with ultimate authority (as keepers of some truth) and give them what they needed: we expected them to engage in a conversation that relied on all voices (teachers, students, authors). Our mistake was in believing that they perceived knowledge as meaning in the making, fundamentally dynamic, a process in which each lends his or her understanding to another. This led us to feel comfortable to add our ideas as the spirit moved us; they found it jarring, unformed, imprecise, even "contradictory."

We thought we were doing a circle dance—"Hava Nagila"—they perceived us as dance partners, pathetically stepping on each other's toes, neither one leading, neither one following, arms flailing to hold our balance. And we were the dance instructors! We didn't know that when we added to each other's ideas it might have been perceived as stepping on toes, that invitations to join the dance circle were perceived as being asked to join a dance that was essentially a "pas de deux." Our failure lay in not challenging early on their notions of what they were seeing and their position to it.

Not all students had this problem. Students who didn't were likely those who held assumptions about knowledge common to ours, students who had experienced classroom discussions in which each member owns his or her own understanding and comes to class to have that understanding deepened and challenged.

Building Relationships with Students

Meeting the student is a large part of teaching, and it doesn't happen in designing the course or in selecting the materials. It happens in the moments of contact between teacher and student: moments that turn on clarity of purpose and the teacher's ability to listen far beyond the words a student may share—to understand intention, to untangle unspoken assumptions imbued in conversations, written work, actions in the classroom. The teacher-student relationship is central, and the presence of two teachers complicates it. We hadn't anticipated this; we were naive to the ways in which this new configuration would influence our ability to enter into effective teaching-learning relationships with the students.

Students wrote frequent response papers to assigned readings. In return we wrote letters to students in response to their thinking. In hindsight we might have assigned each student to one of us as a sort of home base so we could respond consistently to the same students. We had hoped our letters would strengthen bonds between each of us and individual students, but despite our lengthy letters, the personal connections didn't come. The alternate responding disrupted the conversation threading together the oscillating pattern of teacher response—student action, student response—teacher action. Teaching and learning are pulled forward on the backs of such conversations. If we felt the bonds were tenuous, so did they. Again, some students weren't bothered by getting responses from each of us—the same people who on their evaluations expressed the value of two teacher voices.

Teacher as Evaluator

Our intent was to engage in conversation as our students developed their ideas about teaching reading and writing. But for many, their concerns over grades interfered. The issue of teacher as authority/evaluator was exacerbated by the presence of two teachers. Neither of us were novices. Certainly much of what we had learned as teachers of children or as staff developers working in other teachers' classrooms applied to this new teaching situation. When our students were disoriented by the lack of letter grades on their writing (though the criteria for final evaluation were clearly stated in writing on the syllabus), we decided to give them grades as midsemester indicators. When some students expressed indignation at receiving less than an A, we conducted a departmental investigation and found grade expectations had been established outside our course. There is nothing surprising about this: students come into our classrooms with expectations of student and teacher roles that have developed over their long history in school.

Grades have always been the perceptual block keeping teachers from assuming a nonauthoritarian position. Even when clear criteria for grading a paper are set, assigning a grade can stand in the way of open discourse, of risk taking, of creating a context for internal evaluation. When we avoided grading individual steps along the journey of the course, students resented it. And yet when we acquiesced to their need, their concerns flared like a blazing flame. If grading by one teacher feels somewhat arbitrary, it must feel even more random when done by two. For students who already saw us doing a bad fox trot, how much more maddening it must have been to have us give them a grade.

By late spring, with the end of the semester in sight, there was a palpable tension in the class. The students weren't hostile or resistant, not outwardly at least. Rather, they seemed closed to our invitations. And while there were students for whom the class was working, there were enough for whom it wasn't. Our attempts at sparking conversation were too often met with silence. Our invitations for engagement remained unanswered. Two enthusiastic teachers are not enough to maintain spirit and community in the classroom. That energy needs to be accompanied by the students' own enthusiasm and vision. And a synchronicity between the two must exist. By the end of the semester the energy level was pretty low, and when the last class came we were as happy as some that it was finally over.

All classrooms are influenced by the way in which students conceive knowledge, the teacher's ability to build relationships, the authority inherent to the role of teacher. Certainly, none of these issues are particular to coteaching situations. But before either of us fully understood what had taken place, we agreed that had the exact course design been taught by one of us (and it didn't matter which), many of these students would have liked it better. The unexamined gut feeling was that given the way we structured the course, two teachers complicated the matter. What intrigues us still is how a department of education accepted our request to coteach without anyone telling us about the potentials and risks of coteaching. We do not name this as neglect; instead it represents the history of our profession. For most of us the work of teaching is a solitary endeavor lived out behind closed doors.

References

Freire, Paulo. 1991. "The Importance of the Act of Reading." In *The Heinemann Reader: Literacy in Process* (pp. 21–26). Brenda Miller Power and Ruth Hubbard, eds. Portsmouth, NH: Heinemann.

Heath, Shirley Brice. 1982. "What No Bedtime Story Means: Narrative Skills at Home and School." In *Language in Society*, 11, 8: 49–76.

Rosenblatt, Louise. 1991. "The Reading Transaction: What For?" In *The Heinemann Reader: Literacy in Process* (pp. 114–127). Brenda Miller Power and Ruth Hubbard, eds. Portsmouth, NH: Heinemann.

Letting Go of Tradition and Mandates: Creating Curriculum from Students' Lives

LINDA CHRISTENSEN

The first days of school are always a bit tentative in my classroom. I'm never sure how many students on my class list will show up or how many students who registered late will overflow the seating space. Typically, I don't know the students, and they don't know me. I'm a white teacher in a predominately African American school. I'm an aging teacher in a room full of fifteen- to eighteen-year-olds. I'm still that shy girl who hid behind her mother's dress. So I try to ease the tension by using a few routines from the repertoire I've built up over my twenty years in the classroom.

My fourth-block class that year was Senior English, a tracked class where most of the students were short on credits to graduate—as DJ said, "We're not even on the five-year plan"—but long on humor and potential. They came in with their fists up and their chins cocked. They had attitudes. Many of them already had histories with each other—years of playing bully and victim before they ever reached my room. When I asked them to write about a goal, most of them agreed with Chris, "I just want to get the hell out of school."

The first activity was designed to help us learn one another's name. I talked about the importance of naming, discussed Native American, Laotian, Hispanic traditions in naming, the politics of naming and renaming ourselves. I told funny stories about my name. Linda Mae sounds like a cowgirl, I said. I told how I wanted to look like Elizabeth Taylor and I couldn't with a name like Linda. No one laughed. In fact, no one was paying much attention at all. They looked at the clock, the door, slid notes across the desks, whispered to each other. When they did write, it went something like this: My name is Larry. My dad named me. The name poem, my always-worked-in-the-past, sure-fire exercise, failed. The writing and read-around that sometimes takes two days was finished in thirty minutes. No one put any energy into the writing, few people were willing to share what they had written.

The next day, the interview, my second fail-safe exercise, which I discovered in a Writing Project newsletter, failed. Students didn't want to get up and interview each other. They didn't want to write about their names. They didn't want to be in the class, and they didn't want any jive-ass-let's-get-to-know-each-other games or activities. In fact, my class looked like one of the those before shots of an out-of-control class that only superstar movie teachers like Jaime Escalante or Michelle Pfeiffer or Sidney Poitier can bring together with their wisdom and wit.

I moved to a wonderful cooperative learning activity I discovered at an Education Activists conference. I put half the students in an inner circle, facing outward, half in an outer circle facing someone in the inner circle.

"What is this grade school BS?" Chris asked in that kind of whisper that the teacher and the rest of the class are supposed to hear. The class laughed.

"Man, someone is funky. I can't just stand here and smell this for too long," Larry said. The class laughed again.

I decided to keep cool and go ahead. "Okay, outer circle, you have one minute to tell your partner about your best learning experience. Go." I watched the clock. I couldn't hear voices behind me. The minute lasted soooo long. "Now, inner circle, tell your partner about your best learning experience."

"Where do teachers learn these stupid ideas?" Kevin asked his partner. Chris sat down. "I worked late. My feet hurt."

My other five questions were likewise left unanswered. That anyone returned after the first week of school amazed me. If I'd been a student, I would have been scarred for life by the cruelty in the room. I also would have wondered why I had to take this class and why the teacher couldn't "control" it.

When I gave up on getting-to-know-each other activities and plunged into the curriculum, our ninety-minute blocks were painfully long as I failed day after day to elicit response from students other than groans, sleep, or anger. It's hard to build a joyful learning community much less teach the love of literature and the magic of writing when you feel like you're "hoisting elephants through mud" as my friend Carolyn says. I knew it was necessary to break through their apathy and uncover something that made these students care enough to talk, to read, to write, to share—even to get angry.

During those long first days, the only activity that aroused interest was writing about their history as English students—what they liked, what they hated, and what they wanted to learn. They wrote and discussed furiously. Many of these students skulked in low-track classes through most of their education and they were angry about the way their time had been wasted on "meaningless activity." "The teacher would put a word on the board and then make us see how many words we could make out of the letters. Now what does that prepare me for?" But they also hated reading novels and talking about them, because novels "didn't have anything to do with our lives." And they hated writing and being forced to share it with their classmates. The other constant in many of their written responses was that they felt stupid. Some claimed they had been told this directly by teachers in the past.

They had no idea how to participate in a discussion. They talked over one another. They talked at the same time. They interrupted one another and repeated the same story because they hadn't listened. But, for the first time, they got excited and they were talking, telling old stories from middle school, and laughing together instead of hurling insults. I knew what they didn't want: worksheets, sentence combining, reading novels and discussing them, writing about "stuff they didn't care about." But I didn't know what to teach them. I wanted to elicit the excitement and engagement they exhibited when they discussed how teachers had failed to reach them because they were loud and unruly and out of control otherwise. But how? I had one day of success and many days of failure. I decided to try the college course curriculum on this group—the "raise the expectations" approach.

During those initial days of listening to these seniors and trying to read the novel *A Thousand Pieces of Gold,* by Ruthann Lum McCunn, I discovered that what aroused my class was violence. Students weren't thrilled with the book; in fact, they weren't reading it. I'd plan a ninety-minute lesson around the reading and dialog journals they were supposed to be keeping, but only three or four students were prepared.

In an attempt to get them involved in the novel, I read aloud an evocative passage about the unemployed peasants sweeping through the Chinese countryside pillaging, raping, and grabbing what was denied them through legal employment. Suddenly some of the uninterested students saw their own lives reflected back at them through Chen, whose anger at losing his job and ultimately his family forced him to become an outlaw. Chen created a new family with this group of bandits. Students could relate. I had stumbled on a way to interest my students. The violence created a contact point between the literature and the students' lives.

This connection, this reverberation across cultures, time, and gender, belied the students' previous notion that reading novels and talking about them didn't have anything to do with their lives. But it also allowed them to empathize with the Chinese—to learn what another group of people had gone through.

Our school year had opened with a storm of violence in the city. A young man, the brother of a Jefferson student, was shot and killed. Two girls were shot when random bullets were fired on a bus. A birthday party at a local restaurant was broken up when gunfire sprayed the side of the restaurant. So violence—not just in our corner of the city but throughout the entire area—was on the students' minds. Of course, I knew of these events, overheard student conversations, and sat in on discussions with students and faculty members, but I didn't connect this overwhelming issue to the instruction in class. While students were discussing gunshots, I was asking them to write poetry about their names.

When interest generated from the passage was at a fevered pitch, I finally made the right decision: I asked students to write about violence in their own lives. They wrote about violence they witnessed in their neighborhoods. They wrote about getting beaten up by bullies. They wrote about family members who were in gangs or friends who had died. They wrote about their own brushes with violence.

I worried that giving students the invitation to write about violence would glorify it. I don't think that happened. Students were generally adamant that they'd made poor choices when they were involved in violent activities. As one student stated in his essay, "I wanted to be known wherever I went. . . . But I went about it all wrong and got mixed in. . . . Once again I was wrong. It was nothing I had hoped for. Sure I was known and all that, but for all the wrong reasons."

More often students shared their fears. Violence was erupting around them and they felt out of control:

> I fear for my life. I fear for my family's life. I fear for your life. My fear goes deeper than just at school. On the streets it's pitiful because of all the gunfire and killing. I never thought I would have to pack a gat but here it is. I fear being gunned down in the hood. . . .

Through the topic of violence I captured their interest, but I also found a way to get students to talk with one another as real people—not across the screen of a cooperative learning activity designed to get them to know one another, but rather through real conversations that had meaning in their lives. Here they listened and they shared.

Allowing students' interest to help direct the curriculum is not pandering to the student, it is taking the burning concerns in their lives and giving them an opportunity to scrutinize it through the lens of a larger vision.

I didn't have easy answers to these problems in those first weeks, but I had at least broken through their apathy. The students were no longer perfunctorily doing or not doing exercises for me. Not that they were excited about writing an essay about the book, but they were challenged to make it their own, to make it mean something in their lives. They wanted to read their pieces to the class because they wanted to talk about these issues with others. Not every person's story or poem or essay would send the class into heavy discussion, but a number of them did. (And unlike a Hollywood movie, not every person completed the assignments.) Through those papers, students came to know and respect each other.

Because I have internalized the voices of the critics as well as the champions of public education, I sometimes lose my ability to listen to what is affecting my students. I'm too tied up filling the local and state mandates to pay attention to what my students want to know. There are students who sit patiently through boring classes because they believe their reward will come: they will get a diploma, go to college, and have a successful professional career. They know how to jump through the hoops. But there are many students like Chris and DJ who feel impatient with the classroom. School does not engage them. School is so far removed from their lives that they can't see the relevance. As a teacher, my job is to find the electricity that connects my students' lives to the knowledge and skills I'm "required" to teach.

These are days of standarized curriculums and manufactured portfolios. I wonder about these plans made at such great distances from the classroom. How do they take into account Chris, Loris, Shameica, and Larry? How do they listen for the student voice and turn the lesson in a different direction so that students are engaged instead of going through the motions?

Teaching means taking into account the needs of the members of our classroom community instead of mechanically imposing a curriculum. I can sit students in a circle, assign reading and writing activities until the cows come home, but if what I am teaching holds no meaning for the students' lives, I'm just holding them hostage until the bell rings.

Reference

McCunn, Ruthann Lum. 1989. *A Thousand Pieces of Gold.* Boston: Beacon Press.

I Wonder If Real Teachers Have These Problems

CURT DUDLEY-MARLING

F our years ago I took a leave from my duties at York University to teach third grade. Returning to the classroom after thirteen years was a frightening prospect, and I spent considerable time preparing. I frequented bookstores and garage sales to build up a collection of children's books. I reread Nancie Atwell, Lucy Calkins, Donald Graves, Georgia Heard, and Regie Routman. I prepared a schedule and planned units. I even attended a week-long workshop on math manipulatives (not one of my strengths). I did not, however, give any thought to classroom discipline. I think this silence around discipline can be traced to my identity as a whole language teacher. I had come to believe that whole language teachers—because they are progressive, child-centered educators who make every effort to hone students' intentions—were much less likely to have discipline problems.

Reviewing the field notes I kept during my year as a third-grade teacher indicates that discipline was a dominant concern for me throughout the school year. There was nothing I gave more thought to than student discipline and as it turned out, nothing made me feel less adequate as a teacher. I often wondered if real teachers had these problems.

If Good Teachers Don't Have Discipline Problems Was I a Good Teacher?

Catherine, Denise, Crystal, and Fatima were practicing their play in the hall. Some of the boys walking by on their way to the bathroom made fun of them, and several conflicts broke out. Nader broke Denise's wand (he claimed Fatima pushed him). Catherine and Nader got into a pushing match, and Denise scratched Nader and kicked him in the groin. Finally Denise stormed out of class and refused to come back in. So I sent her to the office and, in defiance of me, Connie and Catherine went with her to complain to the principal. It was a pretty awful ending to the day.

(Field notes, January 9, 1992)

Incidents like this one left me feeling helpless and inadequate, wondering if *I* was the problem. I tried hard not to take discipline problems personally, but clearly I did. I even felt responsible when my students misbehaved when they were under the supervision of other adults. What led me to construct a teaching identity for myself that placed such importance on my ability to control my students? Certainly I was legitimately concerned about disruptive or violent behavior that interfered with students' safety and their right to learn. But all teachers must have discipline problems. Why did I find behavior problems so threatening? Part of the explanation lies in popular constructions of the "good" teacher that affected the teaching identity I constructed for myself.

I suspect that *the* defining characteristic of good teachers among the general public is the ability to control their classes. Teachers themselves tend to assess their peers largely in terms of their capacity to establish and maintain control. Presumably, good teachers create the conditions for learning ("all eyes on the teacher") by maintaining appropriate discipline. These are the teachers who "know all the tricks," the ones who have "eyes in the back of their heads." In his book *Among Schoolchildren*, Tracy Kidder (1987) observed that fifth-grade teacher Chris Zajac "could tell, without seeing, not only that a child was running on the stairs but also that the footfalls belonged to Clarence, and she could turn her attention to curing one child's confusion and still know that Clarence was whispering threats to Arabella. She was always scanning the room with her eyes without moving her head, seeing without being seen" (pp. 115–16).

But if good teachers are those who are "in control"—and this begs the question of teachers whose students are well behaved but don't learn much—then teachers who don't exercise the appropriate level of control over their students are not good teachers. Given this equation it's not surprising that I felt so threatened by students' behavior.

Is This the Way *Good* Teachers Behave?

The class was getting out of hand. . . . When Peter kicked Catherine I lost my temper and told him that if he didn't stop I'd let Catherine "kick the hell out of him." I'm plenty embarrassed. . . . I must be very firm with this group but none of them deserves for me to be anything but kind and it's a very bad model in any case. . . . Right now I'm very disappointed in myself.

(Field notes, October 11, 1991)

Linda Christensen (1994) writes: "Over the winter break I read a book on teaching that left me feeling desolate because the writer's vision of a joyful, productive classroom did not match the chaos I faced daily" (p. 1). I often feel that way when I read accounts of teaching. The good teachers I read about are always in control, confident in their abilities, and *fair*. They don't lose their temper. They're never unkind. Tracy Kidder presents Chris Zajac as a teacher who is tough but who earned the respect of her students and colleagues by treating students with kindness and consideration.

If interpersonal qualities like patience, consideration, and warmth are at the heart of good teaching, what am I to make of my own impatience, anger, and frustration?

Sitting here at the computer more than three years removed from my experience as a third-grade teacher, it seems fairly natural to me that teachers will lose their temper from time to time. Try as they may, they will not always be kind. I am willing to forgive my angry lapses as a parent, but I was very hard on myself when I got angry in my classroom. I can only imagine that my construction of the ideal teacher, influenced by the sanitized stories of teaching presented in published research and teacher education, didn't make room for normal human emotions like anger, impatience, and frustration. Many teachers may be denied the professional satisfactions enjoyed by other professionals simply because of their own unrealistic expectations and the certain ambiguities of working in a small space for extended periods of time with twenty-five or more very complicated people.

I Call Myself a Progressive Educator?

I need to go to a point system that rewards students for good behavior. I would like to start tomorrow, but I need to think it out carefully so that I'm able to follow through consistently. I want to withdraw all of our privileges (e.g., using the computer, free choice, library) and make all these (and more) contingent on a good behavior and the points. I've been reluctant to try a point system because I'm worried about the time this management system would take. But the behavior problems we are having are taking far more time. . . . I need to get this under control or my personal goals for the rest of the year could be lost.

(Field notes, January 21, 1992)

Over the next several days I introduced my third graders to a system by which they could earn points for being considerate during circle times and center rotations, participating in gym, and keeping track of their pencils. Students lost points for violence or leaving the classroom without permission. Points were redeemable for such "privileges" as a free-choice activity, playing games on the computer, or having the whole day off from classwork. I also awarded points to the whole class each day that were redeemed for movies, popsicles, field trips, and (once) an ice cream party. Managing the point system was time-consuming. There was, however, a significant improvement in student behavior for the rest of the year, which had a positive effect on my overall outlook on my teaching. On January 23 I wrote in my field notes:

123

The best part of today was that I didn't raise my voice, I didn't threaten anyone, and I didn't really punish anyone beyond asking a few of them to sit out briefly during gym. This system may make it much easier to be consistently kind and considerate.

What interests me about the point system isn't how or why it worked but how it came to be that a holistic educator who has consciously rejected behaviorism as a pedagogical framework came to embrace a quintessentially behavioral solution to discipline problems. I may have "controlled" students' behavior, but I'm not confident that they learned much about getting along in groups as a result. The use of an explicit system of rewards and punishments to control students' behavior echoes the theme in Golding's *Lord of the Flies* that children, if not continually subjected to the controls of a civilizing society, will quickly and certainly revert to their savage selves. Is that how I thought of my students? In my field notes I frequently reminded myself to be considerate and respectful of my students, but I can find nothing considerate or respectful in the conscious, deliberate way I manipulated my students through a token economy. This is not the way I treat my family or friends, nor is it the way I wish to be treated. So how did I come to treat my students this way? How did I come to be a part-time behaviorist?

Although I was willing to ignore the theoretical contradictions of a whole language teacher's implementing a token economy, I was aware of them. I did not, however, give much thought to the ethical problems of token economies. At the time I was just too caught up in *fixing a problem*. I should not, however, be surprised to discover contradictions in my teaching practice. Contrary to some popular myths, people, including teachers, are not always consistent. Recent news accounts indicate that "nice guys" can, for example, abuse their wives or sexually harass their employees. And whole language teachers can sometimes act like behaviorists. Writing this article is the first time I have deliberately and systematically reflected on the ethics of my token economy, and the experience has left me disappointed and embarrassed.

It is my hope that teacher stories that are complicated by the messy reality of life in classrooms can help other teachers make room for the uncertainties, ambiguities, and contradictions that are a certain part of the human experience. Creating teaching identities based on idealized versions of the good teacher will always make it difficult to find much satisfaction in what is already a very difficult—but potentially rewarding—occupation.

References

Christensen, Linda. 1994. "Building Community from Chaos." In *Rethinking Schools, 9.*

Golding, William. 1962. *Lord of the Flies.* New York: Coward-McCann.

Kidder, Tracy. 1987. *Among Schoolchildren.* Boston: Houghton Mifflin.

How Come Nobody's Listening? When Reading Aloud Can Go Wrong

JANICE V. KRISTO

Twenty-five sweaty, red-faced kids swarmed into my classroom after lunch like bees returning to the home hive. The usual havoc after recess, last-minute "let me tell you one more thing" comments, were abuzz in my fifth-grade classroom. It was my first month of my first year teaching a classroom of mostly hardcore behavior problems—a majority of them boys— who from 9:00–3:00 challenged every management strategy in my repertoire.

One strategy, however, that seemed to work well was to read aloud after lunch—a nice quiet way to begin the rest of the afternoon's activities, or so I thought. I had gone through several seating styles, first inviting everyone to sit around me on the floor, as I had seen so successfully accomplished on videos during my teacher preparation program. That worked well for a week (okay, for a day or so). The three Joes in my classroom took this opportunity to practice their own strategies. Let's see what we can do today to drive Miss Kristo over the edge! In those days of little patience, limited experience, and my classroom being next door to the principal's office, it took very little to set me into panic mode. What if the three Joes led a rebellion and everyone walked out of my classroom? (This wouldn't have been without precedent: during the first week of school, one of the more aggressive girls in my room stood up and screamed a rather complex set of colorful words at me and then left the room with several others at her heels.) It was clear that the circle on the floor for Miss Kristo's engaging read-aloud was not going to work for this group, so I had everyone return to his or her desk. I asked that everything be cleared away so that they were ready for this most wonderful time of the day. After several rehearsals all could accomplish this except one of my Joes, who just couldn't sit still unless he had a minimum of three wads of bubble gum in his mouth at one time. Miss Kristo learned a lesson that day—let some things go. After all, he wasn't tormenting anybody; maybe we should just plan to clean multiple layers of gum off the bottom of his desk at the end of the year. (Actually, I think we forgot to do this, so my guess is that twenty-some years later there are still traces of ancient bubble gum stuck to Joe's desk.)

I also wanted to try the recommended practice of setting the stage for the read-aloud by asking some thoughtful questions before reading, talking about the author, the layout of the book, special words that might be challenging, intriguing aspects of the author's style. Needless to say, I over-prepared for read-aloud sessions to guarantee that students wouldn't miss a thing about the special book I had chosen for them. This went well for several days, or so I thought. Every time I was brave enough to look up from my notes everyone was still in his or her seat, I didn't detect any note passing, and desks were still pretty much in the order we started with at the beginning of the day. Ah, the lovely feeling of success! However, on the third day of my focused (and yes, rather rigid) approach, one of my other Joes screamed at the top of his lungs, "So, when are you going to start the next chapter, or are you going to keep on yapping? We want to hear the story!"

Ouch! I felt the pain of defeat and then resentment. Could all those methods texts be wrong, all those reading experts? Why wasn't this working like they said it would? Get me out of here! After a very long pregnant pause, I regained my composure, looked at the clock and thought, Oh, thank God this day will be over in approximately one hour and fifty-eight minutes; I can go home and put my feet in a bucket of hot water and rethink my career plans. I decided to take another approach. I said, "Okay, gang, I'll start reading!" Hoots, whistles, and desk slapping commenced that I'm sure could be heard throughout the three floors of our school!

It dawned on me that I was taking the pleasure out of reading aloud to my students. I never did let go of some talk before reading aloud, but I attempted not to overdo what I thought was a good thing. I became more attuned to student signals that things were not working for them. That was a hard lesson to learn. I needed to balance my agenda of copious notes and questions and let things flow so that I could maintain my real goal—inviting students into the world of good books.

From our conversations I also learned that my students were not used to hearing books read aloud. Apparently, the practice had stopped in their primary years of schooling. I was surprised because even though this was the 1970s, the literature had long supported reading aloud to students of all ages. The lesson here—talk with students about what is working and not working for them—is one of the most powerful educational tools I learned that first year of teaching. I had been more used to taking the challenges of the day home with me and trying to solve them on my own. Our social and academic challenges needed to be tackled and discussed as a group. I found students much more receptive and capable than I had imagined to talk about what made a school day "work" for them. This was also brought home to me in the next scenario.

Choosing just the right book is one of the most significant factors leading to a successful read-aloud. My first choices seemed to be on target. I chose chapter books with mostly male characters involved in lots of action. I felt this would appeal to the boys and the girls would just go along.

One day I began reading a chapter book loaded with descriptions, metaphors, and allegory. The literature reviews agreed that my choice was a good one. But if this book was supposed to be so good, why wasn't anyone listening? Finally, after three days of watching both boys and girls squirm in their seats, I put the book down on my desk and said, "Okay, talk to me about all this squirming." My students looked at me with surprise and a little horror on their faces. I think they thought that I was angry with them. However, I calmly talked about how sometimes our response to a book may be that it's simply boring, and that's all right. Adult readers often choose to put those books aside and start another. We could do just that with this book we were all struggling through; we didn't have to finish it. This admission brought looks of sheer wonderment. We spent the rest of our read-aloud time talking about what kinds of books really excited us and turned us on as readers. (Students were interested to learn that I loved picture books and historical novels.) I know this was the first time these kids had ever had a discussion like this. Together we made lists of the kinds of characters, plots, authors, and writing style that we enjoyed. I asked for recommendations of book titles and selected some of my own. Next, I prepared brief book talks—just enough to whet the appetite—and asked students who recommended titles to do the same. We voted on favorites, and these became our next read-aloud selections.

Our classroom was abuzz with book talk from that day forward—just the kind of literary atmosphere I fantasized about. It was happening so easily, so naturally, and I didn't even have any notes in front of me! Initially, I felt I was giving up some structure and organization. But I stopped worrying when I saw my low-achieving students finally feeling like readers—talking about books as naturally as they talked about the other parts of their lives. Many admitted that they had never been asked questions about their own tastes in reading. After all, they had always been in the low reading group, and teachers told them what to read and how they should think about books.

That day I became hooked on the notion of student talk, choice, and responsibility for decision making, and my students became hooked on talking about themselves as readers.

I Don't Want to See Your Eyes

PENELLE CHASE

Put your head down on your desk, Jeffrey. And I don't want to see your eyes!" On hearing this command, Jeffrey began to inch his head toward the desktop, his brown eyes regarding me saucily. "*Now,* Jeffrey!" His lips curved into the shadow of a smirk, and I lost it. I careened down the aisle to Jeffrey's place in the third row. I put my hand on the back of Jeff's head, and I put—that—head—down on the desk for him. Head met wood with a resounding thunk. I whirled back toward my own desk up front, sick at heart. I will never forget the dart of fear I saw in Jeffrey's eyes as I advanced on him. He kept his head down.

That night I suffered. I was too ashamed and frightened to tell even my husband what I had done. The wait for morning was interminable. I worried that I had damaged Jeffrey irreparably. I was convinced that I would be ignominiously dismissed from my first teaching job. I could not wait to go to school the next day, so that I could apologize to Jeffrey and try again to pick up the pieces of a classroom that was "out of control." But Jeffrey was not in class. My terror increased. I imagined Jeff concussed and in the hospital, his parents preparing to file a lawsuit. There were twenty-seven witnesses to my act of child abuse.

The following morning Jeffrey bounded off the bus and sailed by me ("Hey, Mrs. Chase!") on his way to the playground. It's been twenty-four years, and I can still feel the surge of relief that went through my body. What a wonderful sight! Jeffrey Leclair, unscathed, and no doubt ready for another day of pressing my buttons.

I didn't know much about classroom management early on in my teaching career, but Jeffrey gave me my first lesson. Jeffrey's mocking eyes saw right through me. He saw that I was a sham, that my demands were unrealistic, and he dared to challenge my authority. Our power struggle that went awry that day (as power struggles almost always do) showed me that there had to be a better way of running a class than to say to students: Do it because *I* tell you to do it.

I had had no training as an educator. Maine was desperate for teachers in the late sixties. Holding my brand-new degree in English Literature, I was hired off the street to teach fourth grade. My first year of teaching would count as practice teaching, and I could pick up a few methods courses as I went along. The principal in this rural four-room school was a teaching principal. She was a traditional teacher who did her best to school me in the traditional methods. She counseled me in classroom management. "Do not smile for the first month of school. Don't let the children move a muscle that first month. They will see that you are the boss, and you can ease up ever so slowly as the weeks go by."

However, I was filled with late sixties and early seventies zeal. John Holt and A. S. Neill were my gurus. I was all set to go with individualized instruction, the discovery approach, intrinsic motivation. Learning would be so exciting in my room that the children wouldn't have the time or inclination to misbehave. My principal's very quiet classroom was situated directly below mine, so she heard the chaos that was the result of my innovation and lack of experience. I knew what I wanted to do, but I had no idea how to make it happen. I resorted to trying to control the children, to *make* them mind.

Over the years I never became accomplished in the getting-kids-to-mind techniques. I never mastered the teacher's "look" that is supposed to stop kids dead in their tracks. I have a long list of what hasn't worked in my classroom. There was the *positive reinforcement* school of thought. But saying "I like the way so and so is doing such and such" invariably made me cringe. Extrinsically rewarding students rankled, too. I figured that kids ought to behave because it is the right way to act, not because they are being rewarded for good behavior. *Assertive discipline* demanded that I use check marks on the board to keep track of individual students' transgressions. I was to follow through by meting out an elaborate array of positive and negative consequences. I abandoned that method when I saw it paralyzing the "good" children from any prospect of taking a risk. *Be consistent* was a standard rule of thumb that seemed logical. But even this principle did not work for me. Each incident that came up was different and required a different response. Besides, my gut feeling was that we must encourage students to accept inconsistency. Most recently, I experimented with helping students set their own rules. But I was uncomfortable with the children's rules, which were often even more rigid and more punitive than those that adults think up. Though all these methods effectively controlled students, I never felt sincere in implementing them.

I wish I could pinpoint what *has* worked. I don't want to think that it's a simple fact of now looking old enough to be intimidating, that age has provided me with an authoritarian presence. Somehow, though, during the last several years, the issue of classroom management has been resolved. I don't really know when or how it happened, but I no longer rely on programs, techniques, or stratagems to get students to behave. I no longer manage kids! What am I doing differently?

Six years ago Jane Doan and I began coteaching children in a primary multiage setting. One of our goals early on was to encourage the students to take more responsibility for their learning. Our students stay with us for three or four years, and we assiduously help them in the process of assuming ownership of their education. We have worked hard to tailor our curriculum to provide children with real reasons to learn. We have seen that children *are* intrinsically motivated; they learn eagerly without external rewards. Learning is important in our classrooms; both the adults and the students value it. We talk often about what we have learned and how we have learned it. We are all active participants in our educations.

Over the years as we have refined our program, we have also given children more ownership of their behavior. We have consciously tried to give them room to work on their own social problems. When there are disagreements, I do what I did with my own daughters. I insist that the children stop their play or work and go and talk together. They must figure out a way to carry on that will allow all the parties involved to be happy. I am available to help in this process, but I am rarely asked to assist. The simple activity of talking things through almost always works. The children come to explain their plans to me, feeling good that they have resolved their own problems.

Schools have a long history of control. The teachers in our large elementary school are expected to "report to duty" with their clipboards containing bathroom passes and white detention slips. The whole tone of this kind of supervision is wrong. It sets up a we/they mentality, so that children assume that they have no responsibility for themselves. They are there to be policed. I don't report to recess duty with a clipboard; I saunter outside with my hands in my pockets. If someone has to go to the bathroom or go back inside to get that forgotten jump rope or ball, I trust that child to go into the building without a pass. I have never given a detention slip. Instead, we resolve problems as they arise. Sometimes a child may spend a few minutes sitting and thinking about a better way to act. Sometimes a pair or group of children may spend some time talking out their differences. As in our classroom, we talk a lot on the playground, and we work things out.

For so many years, attempting to control students made me uncomfortable at school. I questioned my own authority as often as the students did. I see now that I've begun to figure out ways to help children take charge of themselves. There was a lesson in the Jeffrey Leclair incident that I ignored for too long. I've thought about Jeffrey often over the years. He was a great kid, full of spunk and imagination. He was a student who struggled with schoolwork but who delighted in life. Jeffrey didn't deserve the treatment he got from me at the end of that harrowing year. I know, though, that he didn't hold it against me.

The Illusion of
Teacher Power

ROSEMARY A. SALESI

Recess duty was never my favorite responsibility. In fact, as a teacher, I never did recess duty until I moved to Maine. Responsibility for two hundred second-to-sixth graders at one time in a large area with little equipment and/or options for activities was frightening. I constantly feared that one of the children would get hurt.

As a beginning teacher, I believed that with my teaching degree I was endowed with a degree of omnipotence. If I requested something, I fully expected the children to comply even if they did so reluctantly. I was the teacher and I was in charge. Over a period of five years of teaching, my sense of omnipotence was tested and it did diminish, but it wasn't until the second graders revolted on my recess duty that I was whittled down to my true size of five-foot-one.

It was a particularly muddy spring in Maine and therefore, when Willard Hillier, the principal, announced that recess would be moved to a new area, I was relieved. The children would be limited to the circular school driveway in front of the main school door. The solution appeared to be a good plan, and as the person on duty alone that day, I thought the plan sounded manageable. Because this area was much smaller than the playground, activities such as a baseball game or soccer game would not be allowed. The area was also small enough that I could move across it in a relatively short time, and there might be fewer disputes to resolve without the team sports.

Willard announced the site change for recess while the children were having lunch. He did not state any new requirements about the children's conduct while on the temporary playground. The children returned to the classroom for their jump ropes, balls, toy cars, dolls, etc. We went out the front door to the circular driveway, and the children quickly spread out on the blacktop that encircled the grassy area where the flagpole stood. This area was also muddy, so I instructed the children to stay on the blacktop. The older children began to spread out to the area at the right of the school where the teachers parked their cars. Fearing that one of their balls might hit a car or a car windshield, I quickly amended my instructions. "Stay on the black-top, the part that's the driveway. Do not, I repeat, do not go near the parked cars in the parking lot." The children were not happy with this restriction. There were really too many children trying to play in a small area. The older boys wanted to play some kind of a ball game and needed more space. They were running regularly into the activities of the smaller children. Jacks went scattering as a sixth grader chased a ball through a group of third-grade girls. This wasn't working out well. I was really missing the second recess-duty teacher and was doing too much yelling: Watch where you throw that ball! Be careful of the younger children! Stop running! The children did not seem to hear or heed my harangues.

My vocal demands increased when the first car driven by a parent attempted to negotiate the circular driveway filled with playing and inattentive children. Despite my frantic hand signals, the parent was determined she would park directly in front of the school door. I struggled to herd my charges out of the way of the car. Before I could speak to the parent about her hazardous driving, I was off to arbitrate a fight between two of the older boys. When the next car appeared, I was on the other side of the driveway, moving the children so the first car could leave. Car after car drove up the driveway, and each driver insisted on parking in front of the school. Not only was my authority diminishing with the children, I obviously had no clout with these parents. To think earlier in the day I had been worried that kids would slide in the mud and break a limb. Now I was terrified that one of them would be hit by a car driven by a rushing parent who expected me just to move these children out of her way. As I repeatedly interrupted a game or moved the jump-rope group to one side of the driveway, the children's negative responses increased. They responded more slowly and even just told me to wait until they finished their turns.

When the recess bell rang, I was exhausted and relieved to be done. "Line up at the front door," I stated repeatedly, as I quickly moved in and among the children. Their response was not too dissimilar to when I asked them to move for the last few cars. "Line up everyone, it's time to go in. The bell rang." I spoke louder with my omnipotent voice, but only small groups of the more timid children moved toward the door.

From behind me, a second grader said, "No! I'm not going in."

"We didn't have any time to play," stated another second grader.

"We don't want to go in," said a third second grader as I tried gently putting my hand on the backs of the students to guide them toward the door.

Wearing my sternest face and using my firmest voice, I again said, "The recess is over and it's time to go in. Line up at the door now!" A few of my own fourth-grade students moved toward the door. I continued to urge with voice and a gentle guiding hand, but their progress was halted when some of the sixth graders joined the second graders' voices.

"We didn't get to play at all."

"We didn't get to finish our game."

"We don't want to go in."

Many of the children watched to see what I would do next. The situation was out of control and I was one moment from hysteria. As I stood my ground, trying to decide what to do next, a more omnipotent person appeared on the front steps of the school, the principal. Taking a grip on myself, I said firmly. "Mr. Hillier, the principal, is waiting for us to line up. Recess is over!"

"Yes, boys and girls, I am waiting for you to line up," insisted Willard. Slowly the older students, who understood the consequences of crossing the principal, began to move forward toward the door. The second graders, seeing the older students heading into the school, reluctantly capitulated to authority and finally joined the rest of the students.

"How did you know I was in trouble?" I asked Willard.

"I didn't. I was just wondering why there were no children moving in the halls and came to take a look."

In our later discussion of "the revolt," Willard apologized for not having some plan to deal with the cars that drove into the circle. Apparently everyone assumed that the visitors had parked in the parking lot. We decided that the rambunctious second graders would spend the next recess with me in my room to discuss appropriate behavior. I also wanted to remind them that I was in charge of the playground, that is, as long as my backup omnipotent figure arrived in time.

There are some stories of my teaching experience I am reluctant to share, but not this story; the day the second graders revolted was the day I learned who was in charge of the school. And over the years I have come to understand that the adults are in charge only if the children are willing to let them be. As long as we do it well and have earned their respect, they will continue to submit to our decisions. This experience has changed my thinking about classroom management and my expectations of myself in a variety of situations. Whether it is a group of children or a number of adults working together, power needs to be shared, problems need to be aired and resolved. When the teacher lets go of the concept of full authority, it also means the teacher no longer needs to be able to cope with all the problems. It is okay to admit you don't know how to solve a problem and seek help. Today if I were in that same situation, I would send a child to find the principal and let him deal with the cars. I would not try to be everywhere on that playground solving all the problems. The lessons I learned from those spirited second graders continue to remind me that I am not omnipotent nor do I want to be.

An Incorrect Correction

CYNTHIA MCCALLISTER

*If only I had the confidence of being
a good teacher. But I'm not a good
teacher. I'm not even an appalling
teacher. I don't even claim to be a
teacher at all. I'm just a nitwit
somehow let loose among children.*

Sylvia Ashton-Warner

Andrew Wright was as quick as a whip. When I think of him now, six years later, I vividly recall his wide, lively brown eyes behind dark bone-rimmed glasses. His look usually conveyed an undercurrent of mischief combined with wisdom that, to me at the time, seemed unusual in a child of his age. I met Andrew on my first day as a classroom teacher. It took a few short days for me to recognize that he was not a typical fifth grader. Being a new teacher, I had neither the benefit of experience nor a teacher's intuition to help me identify or name the subtle nuances of Andrew's gifts. My abilities to observe and assess children were more or less primitive hunches at that point in my career. Through rudimentary judgments, I assigned children more or less into the simple categories of *low, medium,* and *high.* Andrew was the highest of highs.

In any of my subsequent years as a teacher I would have found Andrew's wit and brilliance appealing and entertaining—an asset to my classroom community. But as it was, being a brand-new teacher who lacked confidence and skill, entrusted with the responsibility of providing an education to a child prodigy who seemed to match my intellect on many levels, Andrew kept me uncomfortably on my guard. In spite of my initial lack of confidence, as time passed that first year I grew accustomed to working side by side with a ten-year-old "genius" who frequently proved to be a quicker thinker than me.

After the initial marathon weeks of getting organized and accustomed to the demands of teaching, I became content with the set routines and habits

I had carved into the form of a predictable, daily instructional itinerary, one element of which was a weekly spelling quiz. Every Monday I introduced a new list of words, assigned pages of homework from the textbook to be due throughout the week, and on Friday gave my students a spelling quiz. At the time, I felt comfortable with that routine. There were some drawbacks, the main one being the huge mound of papers that needed my constant attention each evening. At one stage during my first year as a teacher I was correcting on the average sixty pages of student assignments each night. Typically, I would sit down with my stack of papers and begin plodding through them, pen in hand. I would move into a trancelike state akin to that when I stand at the kitchen sink peeling potatoes and gazing out the window. The nightly task was tedious and uninteresting. But at the time, I was at a loss for an alternative. The routine of my teaching day was, on the surface, quiet and industrious by virtue of busying my students with a constant barrage of assignments.

By mid-October I was feeling comfortable with my teacherly persona and assured that I was managing the education of my students nicely. When parent conference night arrived, I found myself a little nervous, but any hesitation was kept at bay by my emerging confidence. I arrived at school early in the evening, prepared for my first conference. By the rural Maine standards that prevailed among the staff of my school, I had dressed lavishly for the occasion in a plain navy wool skirt and a dressy blouse. I thought the outfit made me look teacherly and professional, if only slightly overdressed. Above all, I wanted to portray an image of competence and skill—I wanted to instill a sense of reassurance in the minds of my students' parents that their children were in good hands.

The meeting with Andrew's mother was my second of the evening. My first conference had gone smoothly, and Andrew was such a bright student, I expected my meeting with Andrew's mom to go well. Mrs. Wright followed me into my big, empty classroom. I was struck by how strongly she resembled her son. She had the same all-knowing look that convinced me of the presence of deep, interior thoughts. She also had a very no-nonsense approach to casual conversation, which, within minutes, made me feel uneasy and guarded. It wasn't long before I began to feel self-conscious and insecure.

"It's a pleasure having your son in my class," I offered. "He is a quick thinker and offers a positive contribution to class discussions." She nodded in agreement. It soon became obvious that my insights were not original; I'm certain she'd heard similar comments each year at her son's conferences. "He has such a wonderful sense of humor," I continued. "And he is very well liked by his classmates." The conference limped along. I was anticipating our final good-bye when Mrs. Wright made it clear the conference was not finished.

"Oh? You have a concern?" I respond in a feigned tone of casual competence. Suddenly, Mrs. Wright reached into her purse and produced one of Andrew's recent spelling tests I had graded. I glanced at the top where I had written: "100%." But below, three out of ten words were circled in pencil. I suddenly felt confused and off guard. "I don't understand," I muttered. In a firm and subtly accusing tone Mrs. Wright pointed out that Andrew had obviously misspelled three words on his spelling test. I had overlooked them, giving him a perfect score. Mrs. Wright went on to explain her concern: Andrew is a bright boy, but weak in some areas. Because of his brilliance he is often eased of the pressure to achieve, held to a different standard than the rest of his classmates. He needs instruction and guidance, just as any other child. She was justified in her criticism; and she waited for an explanation, pinning me down with her serious eyes.

I felt my stomach turn and my face flush. In my mind's eye I could see myself, in my tidy classroom, overdressed in a navy wool skirt and a dressy blouse, feigning confidence and competence, and suddenly having my cover blown by one of my student's parents. I felt stupid and pathetic! I wanted the ground to open up and swallow me. But I also realized I needed to be professional and at least make some attempt to save face in this unpleasant situation. How could I have overlooked three misspelled words, giving a perfect score to a child who deserved an average one? I apologized and offered my excuse . . . I had simply overlooked the errors. Mrs. Wright knew, and so did I, that my excuse wasn't adequate.

The incident of the incorrect correction occurred because I relied on routines that allowed me to blindly assign and reassign students into categories. It came early in my teaching career and derived from the unreasonable routine of weekly spelling tests, which I abandoned soon after. But the development of innovative practices hasn't delivered my teacher's subconscious from the dangerous ghost of Andrew and unbridled assumptions. In fact, regardless of how progressive my teaching becomes, I find myself continually exorcising him from my instructional practices. While my approaches to and philosophy of teaching have changed over the years, the newer, modified routines I currently embrace also fall victim to mindlessness, complacency, and routinization.

I'm faced with a continual challenge to structure enough routine into the classroom experience to support higher levels of thinking and learning for my students and myself. But the danger arises when I blindly or thoughtlessly embrace routines, allowing them to resemble tracks that take my students and me over the same terrain, day in and day out, steering us clear of the unexpected surprises that take learning in new and necessary directions. When my teaching routines and habits allow me too easily to slip into a potato-peeling frame of mind . . . that's when I know the ghost of Andrew lurks around the corner.

Reference

Ashton-Warner, Susan. 1963. *Teacher.* New York: Simon & Schuster.

The Boob Thing

BRENDA MILLER POWER

ritics attack university faculty as politically correct and ivory-tower irrelevant. Those of us who try to prove these critics wrong by making our classes connect with life beyond the campus sometimes show only how accurate their perceptions may be.

In the fall of 1992, I decided to explore the quincentennial of Columbus's entry into America as a theme in my undergraduate literacy methods class. In a state that is 98 percent white, our campus sits less than five miles away from one of the three Indian reservations in the state. It is an uneasy relationship. As part of a treaty agreement, the campus provides full scholarships to Native Americans with a certain percentage of Native American blood. There is a lot of resentment among some students about this arrangement, especially since tuition rates have more than doubled in the past decade. In return, the Natives who live on the reservation resent the visits by college faculty and students that make them feel like exotic animals in a zoo.

I thought considering Columbus's place in history through multiple sources—children's and adult literature, videotapes, teaching resource guides from the *Rethinking Schools* organization—would show us all the challenges of presenting and respecting multiple views in the classroom and society. I hadn't thought enough about how we might deal with all those resentments simmering beneath the surface—not in mythical classrooms my students would lead someday, but in our own.

In mid-October, I noticed a panel discussion was taking place on campus to discuss the quincentennial. Luckily (I thought!), the discussion would occur right in the middle of our three-hour class period. Our class made plans to attend. If I had read the fine print on the poster, I might have been concerned about the militant Marxist group sponsoring the event. If I had been more aware, I might have been even more concerned that the Native Americans who were speaking were affiliated with a radical separatist Native American group.

The room was fairly large, accommodating about one hundred and fifty people. On the morning of the panel discussion, my dutiful students arrived early. Mostly women, mostly white, we settled into the most comfortable chairs in the back of the room and listened to the speakers, one male, the other female. What we heard was a rant in stereo about how these two were offended that we had even shown up. The Native American culture was for Natives, we were told, and we had no right to it. We were usurping their rituals, their beliefs, and trivializing them with our sweathouses and chants. In return, we had poisoned their lands and raped their people.

When it came time for questions from the audience, a number of people stood up and asked how connections could be made, how these walls of anger could be broken down. There was no way to undo the damage, the panelists said. A Native American woman in the audience stood up and said she was offended. The male panelist said she was free to leave.

But the pivotal moment for my young, white, middle-class female students came when the four-year-old son of the woman on the panel began to whimper at her feet. The woman continued to answer a question as she unbuttoned her shirt, pulled her breast out, and began to nurse her son. I feared I would have to move through the room and nurse my own students with smelling salts, because many of them looked pale and ready to fall out of their seats.

When we met back in our classroom after the panel discussion ended, I knew we needed some time for open talk about what we saw. I asked the students what things they were thinking about. "Well, I'll never forget the boob thing!" one exclaimed. Other classmates nodded and laughed. "I mean, she just whipped it out there!" Another student was firmer in her response. "We can laugh, but I'm not laughing at what I heard. I think it's crap that we give these people full scholarships to our campus and then they act like that!"

Another student sitting three seats down, a quiet young woman named Noreen, burst into tears. "I listen to that shit from you people every day I live on this campus, and I'm sick of it. I didn't come from the Reservation to hear this!" And with that, most of the class realized they had a Native American sitting in their midst. She had chosen to remain silent about her heritage up to that point in the semester.

Somehow we got through that last half hour of class. I was babbling as fast as I could about needing to be aware of diversity in our midst and the incredible need in the state for more Native teachers.

When I left the classroom, I walked straight to my dean's office to ask him what I should do. I talked with Noreen that night. She had walked straight to the office of Native Affairs. The next class, we had a long discussion about what had happened. There were profuse apologies, more tears, some Native guest speakers scheduled to present alternative views to what we had seen on the panel, and we were a close community again by the end of the semester. We learned you don't dive too deep, that the language of the classroom shouldn't mirror the language students use to discuss issues in their homes.

What no one but me knows to this day is that there were two Native American women in that class. The other Native student, Emily, came into my office the first week of class and talked about her middle-class upbringing and what studying the theme meant to her. She and her parents laughed at her cousins from the suburbs with their 25 percent Native American bloodlines who rushed to get their full scholarships to the university. Her family all felt it was a scam, but it wasn't something Emily felt comfortable discussing in class.

What I learned about my teaching, my students, and the place of debate on college campuses today through this experience still troubles me. When I walked out of the class after the confrontation, I was worried about the feelings of my students. But I was also worried about being sued for creating a hostile environment. I read the *Chronicle of Higher Education,* and I see how often careers are destroyed or at least set back by one controversial incident in a classroom. I know three colleagues who have been sued by students for less.

I thought campuses were the place for open debate, for probing deeply every controversial issue we face as a society. It wasn't that we didn't still discuss Columbus through the rest of the semester, but we tread carefully, skimming the surface of the issues. In that wonderful shorthand students develop, the panel discussion was referred to as The Boob Thing throughout the final weeks of the semester. The Boob Thing was a microcosm of everything wrong with the atmosphere in my classroom. What should have been a natural act, a choice among many for mothers, became an in-your-face defiant public display for my students. Voices on each side became more shrill. Offense led to students shutting down, and there was no healthy way for us to discuss options and opposing views without nasty exchanges and tears.

In the fraternity and sorority houses that ring our campus, students fuel one another's anger about scholarships for minority groups. As she walks to class, not a week goes by in which Noreen doesn't hear some group of students ahead of her on the sidewalk denigrating her people. And Emily from the suburbs is silent in class. She saves her views for the dorm room she shares with friends.

In the midst of the controversy, when I wondered if my class would ever come together as a community again, I received the latest newsletter from the largest service organization for teachers in my field. Though the membership of this organization is mostly public school teachers, the organization itself is run primarily by university faculty. In the Letters to the Editor section, there was a harsh and angry letter from an academic criticizing the professor who serves as a chair of a committee. The committee chair, a well-known feminist, had been quoted in a previous newsletter as saying that it was the job of her committee to "disseminate information about gender differences in classrooms." The offended letter writer was shocked that her colleague would use a phallologic word like *disseminate.* If *phallologic* isn't in your vocabulary, just stop a moment. Break it down and think about it. If a word like *disseminate* must go, so too must we rid ourselves of *seminar* and *seminal ideas* . . . I bet we could come up with quite a long list. And while we academics are breaking it down, thinking about it, and attacking each other over the roots of words, our students may literally be telling each other they are full of shit when it comes to discussing issues of race and culture.

In my class, we talk and talk and talk. We talk about the difference between whole language philosophy and practice, about the benefits of group book discussions versus individual reading of texts. The air fills with words as sharp as noodles, rarely cutting into the views that unite and divide our campus. As I teach, I meter out controversy, the things that really matter, in teaspoon doses. I'm diligently swimming my laps in an ever-smaller pool. And I wonder how often during those late-night debates in the student housing throughout campus the words "But my professor says" are ever heard. Probably as often as we deserve to have them heard.

Ma$_4$

DOLORES MILLER

lmost twenty years ago, I was teaching chemistry to college prep students in a rural high school in western New York. At that time, I believed that teaching was presenting information and learning was the result of a lot of hard, lonely work. My lessons usually included some lectures, chemistry demonstrations, and lab work. I had completed a traditional lecture lesson on how to write chemical formulas, using correct symbols and subscripts. We tried some formulas together in class, but my students needed more experience. To practice this skill they were assigned a rather lengthy list of formulas to calculate overnight and turn in the next day.

As I was grading that rather routine chemistry homework assignment the next night, I came to an answer Ma_4PO_2 as the formula for magnesium phosphate. Since the correct answer is $Mg_3(PO_4)_2$, the subscripts were obviously wrong. But even stranger, there is no element with the symbol Ma. I marked it wrong and finished grading that paper. I thought no more of it until a few papers later, I found that same answer again. I did a double take, went back through the pile, and found the first paper. These two papers were identical in every way, with the same mistakes and even the same omissions! I gave them both a grade of zero and wrote on one "Just like George's" and on the other "Just like Tom's."

This was years before I used cooperative learning techniques and knew the value of collaboration. Back then, it was all, Keep your eye on your own paper, do your own work, work alone. The excuse "we worked together" was unacceptable, and I took pride in cautioning my students that the zero I gave to the "copyee" was as round as the one I gave to the "copier"!

I continued to grade the assignment. Soon I found another exactly the same. I gave another zero and wrote "Just like Tom's and George's" and added Bill's name to the papers of George and Tom. Kim's paper soon joined the pile.
"Just like

Tom's,
George's,
Bill's."

I found another and another.

"Just like
Tom's,
George's,
Bill's,
Kim's,
Sue's,
Mark's."

I was distressed to see this many people copying homework. The pile continued to grow, and I patiently continued to add names to the list at the top of each student's paper.

"Just like
Tom's,
George's,
Bill's,
Kim's,
Sue's,
Mark's,
Mary's,
Pete's,
Jim's,
Linda's,
Gail's,
John's,
Jenny's,
Barbara's."

I began to be very curious how all this had started. I studied the magnesium phosphate answers a little closer. No clues came to light.

"Just like
Tom's,
George's,
Bill's,
Kim's,
Sue's,
Mark's,
Mary's,
Pete's,
Jim's,
Linda's,
Gail's,
John's,
Jenny's,

Barbara's,
Dave's,
Phil's,
Mike's,
Bob's,
Ruth's,
Joan's,
Pat's,
Kathy's."

Now there was hardly enough room at the top of the papers for all the names, but I was determined to finish what had become quite a project. No longer angry, I was amazed at the scope of the student network.
"Just like
Tom's,
George's,
Bill's,
Kim's,
Sue's,
Mark's,
Mary's,
Pete's,
Jim's,
Linda's,
Gail's,
John's,
Jenny's,
Barbara's,
Paul's,
Rick's,
Nancy's,
Sharon's,
Matt's,
Ron's,
Sherry's,
Kelly's,
Scott's,
Tim's,
Steve's,
Anne's,
Chris's,
Don's,
Irene's,
Ed's."

As I finished grading I studied the papers before me. It appeared that someone had carelessly written the g on Mg without a distinct tail. The next person had copied it as an *a,* and thus it began. A third of all my students, spanning four classes, had participated. This was before the Internet, but they had formed quite a web.

The next day as I passed back the papers I watched the expressions on their faces as they read the lists on the top and compared papers: embarrassed grins, heads straining to see who had been caught. They were not so much amazed that they had been caught copying as they were that I had figured out who everyone was and taken the time to write it down. Nobody protested, but finally a courageous student asked what tipped me off. When I told them about the nonexistence of element Ma they were impressed that I showed more diligence in completing my work that they had in completing theirs.

I didn't realize it, but for the students on the list, that wasn't the end of the assignment. A few days later a new element mysteriously appeared on the large periodic table that dominated the back wall of the classroom. After the last element block on the periodic table, there are always some blank blocks for heretofore undiscovered elements. Up to this point the last element was number 103, Lw. Now there was a new element 104, called Ma, on my periodic table. It was printed meticulously to look exactly like all the other elements. When I asked my students about it, they said, Well, now there *is* an element Ma and notice that it has a mass of 0.000, just like our grades!

I no longer teach writing formulas as I did then. The art of teaching has changed and so have I. After an introduction with examples, the students work together in cooperative groups. They play with paper clips and other manipulative devices to build compounds, accommodating their particular learning styles. They practice writing formulas with their classmates. The homework assignment is not as lengthy as twenty years ago. When they bring in the homework the next day, they are encouraged to compare answers and to help each other understand and correct mistakes before they turn it in. This collaboration, quite different from the type students used when the element Ma was discovered, results in more learning.

That periodic table, with the mysterious element Ma, was on the wall for many years and new students in chemistry class would often ask about it. I would reply with a smile, "Well, it's a long story, but since you asked . . ."

Testosterone Test Fails College Students

MICHAEL GINSBERG

I figured a unit on *gender* issues would be sexy.

I figured community college students would find *gender* an intellectually stimulating and personally relevant topic to study—one in which personal experiences would provide a rich source of background knowledge.

I figured debates on *gender* differences would be lively and generative.

I figured wrong.

Blame it on stubbornness. Blame it on testosterone poisoning. Blame it on the bossa nova. Whatever the reason, I persisted with a unit on gender issues for four semesters. Four unsuccessful semesters. But I'm finally giving up.

If this case study were a murder mystery, it would be called *Death by Good Intentions.* In other words, "it seemed like a good idea, but. . . ." Whatever the title, the gender unit is dead. As I plan a replacement unit—full of good intentions, of course—I've determined that an autopsy is indicated.

First, some history. I teach reading at an urban community college. Most of my reading courses are designed for underprepared students who demonstrate few successful strategies for meaningful reading. I also teach a course called College Reading, CMS 185, which is designed for students who *should* be able to handle college-level reading assignments. The course is an elective that has been poorly defined by the school administration and poorly understood by the faculty who teach it and the students who enroll. Some of the students are graduates of developmental reading courses who have been advised to continue to take reading courses; some are students who need an elective and figure something called College Reading won't be too demanding; some simply stumble into the class, thinking it is an English course.

CMS 185 is home for the gender unit, wedged in between a unit on essays and a unit on short stories. All three units include many invitations to respond in writing to the texts; there are no conventional tests.

The essay unit has evolved into a successful experience, and the short stories have always been popular. In each case, students select their readings from a text set with twenty to thirty readings and write responses that are both personal and text-based. In addition, we read common texts in class and examine sample student responses to build model responses.

The gender unit was different. Everyone got the same twenty-page chapter from a college psychology textbook. The chapter covered standard material on conventionally recognized gender differences, social and biological explanations for those differences, and implications. Using a variety of strategies, students tried to develop a solid understanding of and a clear set of notes from the chapter; they also read essays related to gender issues and tried to decide where the essays fit with the material in the textbook chapter. For a final assignment, I gave them a newspaper article about differences in male and female membership and performance in high school academic quick-recall teams. Imagining themselves as consultants to the school board, they were to explain the gender differences on the teams and recommend a course of corrective action. Their responses were supposed to demonstrate creativity and an understanding of the textbook chapter.

Based on my observations and the formal and informal feedback I received from my CMS 185 students, the gender unit was the least popular of the three units in the course. In fact, the last time I taught the course in this configuration, student evaluations included *no* substantial criticism of the essay and short story units and *much* criticism of the gender unit.

Here are a few unedited criticisms of the unit, as they appeared in anonymous course evaluations:

- "I think you could improve this section by creating a different approach to looking for the correct points in the gender section."

- "I found a lot of things that was helpful, but I did not like this section at all. Plus it was very boring."

- "I didn't like this unit it was to indepth."

- "I liked everything except the gender text. It was confusing in some parts explaining what I read. I grew tired of talking about gender and therefore did bad on the test."

- "This was hell. I didn't like it, but I did learn from it."

What did *I* learn from this unit and from the responses of my students? Here are problems that I've identified:

- Subject Matter, or *Know Your Audience*. Stated simply, my students did not find the subject of gender differences as interesting as I had anticipated. Even a humorous—at least I thought so—essay by Alan Alda on testosterone poisoning met an underwhelming response.

- Text Choice, or *Trust Your Audience.* This is most troublesome to me, philosophically. I believe—strongly—that readers have more successful experiences when they choose the text(s) that they read, for their own purposes. In both the essay and short story units, students *did* choose most of the texts that they read. In the gender unit, everyone read the same textbook chapter. I wanted a common experience, but I think we paid a high price.

- Text Quality, or *Know What You've Got.* Not only was the text selected by me, but it was, in current terminology, an inconsiderate text. It took three semesters for me to realize how inconsiderate the text was, and I tried to turn that to advantage during the fourth semester by demonstrating strategies to salvage meaning from such texts. No deal.

- Assignments. (See *Know Your Audience.*) This was another tough one. After two semesters, I realized just how much trouble my students were having with the text. So I slowed down the process, adding a number of supportive assignments that were designed to help the students assess their understanding of the material and the quality of their responses. During the last semester, I even added team projects. I never did achieve a balance between ample demonstration and comfortable pacing. In short, we either proceeded too quickly—in which case much of the class was left behind, or too slowly—in which case much of the class was left sleeping.

- Assignments II, or *Dessert First.* I wanted my students to muck around with the texts, find ways to make sense of them, and create new understanding from them. But they became painfully bogged down with surface-level understanding and I became preoccupied with finding ways to help them understand what they were reading. As a result, my assignments began to resemble little more than study strategies, and the potentially attractive final assignment—the one that I designed to invite application, creativity, and divergent thinking—came too little, too late. In retrospect, I think I went about structuring this unit backward.

So what am I left with? First, a huge file of gender material that I've clipped and saved for the past nine years—since I first tried teaching a gender unit as a graduate student. It's the classroom equivalent of uncooperative bread dough; after four hours of mixing, kneading, and waiting, what do I do when it still refuses to rise?

The file is an albatross. It is hard for me to let go of material that *seems* good. I've invested so much time, energy, and ego in collecting and using the stuff, and it keeps coming. As I write this, I'm salivating over a *New York Times* article about researchers who are questioning conventional wisdom concerning the role of testosterone in "male" behavior. Hmmm. Maybe if I just change the textbook for the unit and . . .

I'm also left with a hole in my syllabus—and the sense that I *do* need to fill that hole with something involving the reading of college textbooks. (This *is* a college reading course, after all.) I'm thinking of adapting a high school history assessment exercise as the basis for a replacement unit. I intend for the unit and the assessment to be more authentic than the gender unit, even if it still involves an assigned text.

Finally, as I plan this new unit, I'm left with some important lessons:

- I've become more modest in assuming I know what will interest my students. I'm still surprised that the gender unit didn't sell, but I don't think it will ever again take me so long to give up.

- Although I understand that I will always have to balance my theoretical positions with the realities of teaching, I will try to be more careful about the compromises I make. Given the need that I've identified to work through a common text, I'm now convinced that I can offer multiple invitations and a selection of secondary texts to expand the number of choices within the unit. I sacrificed too much this time.

- Faced with an inconsiderate text in the future, I think I can avoid shrinking the focus of my students to the point where they are simply strip-mining for facts. For example, I envision starting the replacement unit with a broad, general and—I hope—attractive invitation attached to the history textbook section. From the start, students will know their purpose for reading the text; they won't have to first extract meaning and then apply their understanding to some broader purpose. With a purpose in mind, I can help students devise strategies for using the text.

- By *starting* the unit with an articulated purpose, I think I stand a better chance of helping my students stay directed. Without the vision of an end point as a starting point, my students had trouble moving themselves along. By laying out that vision from the start, I will be less likely to lose students along the way as I make midcourse corrections.

Not a bad salvage operation. These have been painful lessons, but I don't know if I would have learned them without experiencing the failures. I'm also not sure it had to take four tries, but I'll leave that issue behind. Two steps are important now: drop the old and apply the lessons to the new.

Oh, one more thing: anyone want to buy an eight-inch file on gender . . . cheap?

How I Learned to Love the Hard Drive

JEFFREY D. WILHELM

Hypermedia!

The word itself fairly sang to us. "And besides," I told Paul, "anything with the word *hyper* in it belongs in a middle school!"

Paul Friedemann and I had been team-teaching seventh grade together for several years. For some time, we had been searching for ways to help students find, explore, and create their own knowledge. We had helped our students write historical novels, create classroom dramas, and videotape documentaries about local issues. Now it was time to move our student designers into the computer age. "The computer is an important way to extend our human abilities, and kids need to know how to use them for their own purposes" was something I wrote in my journal as we discussed our incipient project.

When we explained that we would help small groups of students pursue their own research questions about culture and create their own hypermedia documents to teach others, the response was immediate. "It will be chaos," our computer teacher told us. "You want them to think and create with the computer instead of using it for fun," said a university professor we consulted. "Don't think the kids will thank you for this."

"Remember—every educational experiment is doomed to succeed!" I told Paul, and he laughed. This was a catchphrase we often repeated to each other, and Paul was probably thinking of some of our previous "successful" experiments.

Informed by our prior pedagogical snafus, we proceeded carefully. We decided that we would first introduce our students to hypermedia through set cards, which we would design. Students would fill in a series of cards about their own personality and family, learning how to type information on fields and backgrounds, scan in photos, draw and create graphics, record music, and create buttons and links between the cards. Only at the end of the project

149

would we allow the students to create one or two cards of their own and link them to the hyperstack that we had essentially created for them. This seemed a reasonable first step toward our ultimate goal of student teams pursuing their own research questions and creating sophisticated hypermedia documents to teach others.

So I created a personality profile stack and began to load it on our lab's computers. Our district technician suggested that we simply load it on the fileserver, so students could access the hyperstack on the local area network. Voilà! We were ready for the computer age!

Disaster struck the first day. When we turned on the lab computers, we found that the fileserver was down. I could *not* believe it! The well-made lesson plan and finely tuned student enthusiasm were laid to rest. We had to load the hypercard application and the stack we had designed on each individual computer, which turned out to provide faster access anyway—and we didn't have to worry about the fragile fileserver's going down. But a whole class period went to waste, and there was the gravelly taste of gnashed teeth underneath my tongue by the end of the period.

Then came the floppy disc problems. We thought that because Hyper-Card automatically saves files, we would be fine on this score. We thought that because floppies have lifetime warranties, they would last through one middle school semester. We were wrong—and not for the last time. Joe took his disc home in his jeans pocket and it went through the washing machine. Several discs were lost, and several broke down. Some students unwittingly flipped the lock tab on the disc, making it "read only" and not able accept new data. (It took me two whole class periods to figure out that one.) One whole class reformatted and erased another class's set of discs along with a week's worth of their work. Three disc gates were intentionally opened and the discs vandalized with a pencil. I could feel something growing deep inside me, something I imagined to be a gargantuan stomach-eating ulcer.

So we assigned students to work on particular computers and asked them to automatically save their work on a student file folder on the hard drive. They then were to make a backup copy on floppy disc each day, which had to be kept in the computer room. In this way there was always one—if not two—relatively safe copies of their latest work available.

After a week I wrote: "The first thing I've learned is that using a computer is like marriage. It's going to give you your best *and* worst moments. You can't foresee what will happen. The only thing you can count on is having to solve problems you never ever foresaw! There is going to be failure, sound, and fury and a lot of it is going to signify just about nothing. . . . I'm frustrated, the kids who have lost data are upset, sometimes I'm so lost I don't know where to turn . . . which makes me wonder why I wandered into the computer lab in the first place!"

In the next week, a different brand of anarchy reigned. Some students had just been provided with too much, too soon. It seemed there were thirty hands in the air all of the time, connected to squirming bodies running off at the mouth with comments like, It *doesn't* work! and HELP ME! When I would hear the same problem twice, I would announce a solution. They wouldn't listen to me, so busy were they with yelping, It doesn't WORK! I wondered if Indiana Jones would swap me his snake pit for this dungeon of squirming, hormone-geysering, computer-freaked twelve-year-olds. But I persevered, and together we teachers designed Help Sheets and taped them next to every computer and on top of the optical scanner. Still I was running from student to student. Sometimes I would encounter a new problem, and the student and I would pore through our HyperCard manual together. More often, I was simply barking, "Look at your Help Sheet!" By the end of each class I would be panting like a big red dog running in the yard on a hot day. Three computers broke down, and in some classes I had to put two students on a single machine.

Then students began to discover special effects and features. That was a whole new kettle of fish! They would be creating exploding screens and closing barn doors and making flip card animations instead of pursuing the content of the assignment. Though I try to operate with a minimum of rules, I made a new one: Before you can create a new card, you have to complete a Card Plan Sheet and have it approved.

Some students discovered the control panel on the computer. Programs froze; dirty messages appeared on the desktop patterns. Some students gave themselves file passwords that they promptly forgot. They were therefore forever frozen out of their file. Some days I felt like a little primal scream therapy might be in order.

In my journal that week I wrote two new catchphrases: "A little knowledge is a dangerous thing—especially on the computer!" and "The computer certainly can extend our human abilities—if there are any abilities to be extended!"

Privately, Paul and I both harbored thoughts about not even attempting our big plans for a cultural journalism stack. Publicly, we agreed that we needed to do another HyperCard project before the Big One, and we set about planning a small student-designed stack that would report on a psychology topic. Individual students would design a four- to six-card stack to be used by other students.

During this second project, we again had problems, but they were generally new problems. For example, so kids could design their own cards the User level had to be set at 5 or 6, yet our computers automatically opened on a lower User level. Therefore the kids were locked out from creating cards. So we had to solve that problem. Students lost the menu bar or found they were working on a background instead of a card—which had surprising effects on every card on their stack. And we began to have more content problems: fuzzy research questions, trouble finding information on the topic, specious links between cards, that kind of thing. Though we weren't so philosophical at the time, the new failures, frustrations, and problems all indicated learning progress.

In January, when our cultural journalism groups began to design hyper-stacks of up to 150 cards, most of the computer problems receded into the background. It had taken two projects and a lot of patience to learn the computer tools, but all 120 of our students had done it. We now began to work in earnest to help our students ask questions, organize and link information, develop critical standards, and design exciting cards.

The payoffs for the pandemonium of the fall began to roll in. The higher levels of success were accompanied, as always, by more sophisticated problems. Motivation was extremely high; the computer lab was filled from an hour before school until we chased our students out somewhere between 4 and 5 P.M. At this point, the kids began to surpass us as hypermedia experts. Some students learned how to do drag-animation and create pop-up fields. They then taught their friends. If we found a new student who wanted to learn about these tools, we said, Talk to Tony. He's the expert. And they did. And Tony taught them what he knew. Expertise became distributed throughout the classroom, and students turned to each other for advice.

The students began to indicate that they were thinking about multiple aspects of their document, conceiving of their card stack as a whole, considering their purpose and how it would serve their audience, looking ahead to what they wanted to do next. Kids were continually on the phone with informants, watching videos about their culture, and revisiting the library in the quest to more fully answer their research questions.

There continued to be problems: research questions too big, too small, too fuzzy, or too uninteresting; problems finding information and informants; poorly designed cards; special effects that served no purpose. But the students themselves were often becoming aware of their problems. They were beginning to construct and apply their own critical standards.

At the end of the year, I wrote, "Paul and I realized that we were modeling learning and problem solving in the classroom as we dealt with all of the problems that came up and as we helped students deal with the problems that came up for them. We also know that we are dealing with an important educational problem: how to make technology an ally that serves our curricular needs. How can a teacher keep up with rapidly evolving technology and still do a competent job of teaching? How can a teacher teach *and* solve the problems that arise with computers? What kind of support do teachers need to implement new technologies? Paul and I agree that we would not have attempted much less been able to finish these projects without each other's support."

Paul wrote, "Using technology helped us open up to change and become more adept at changing. We were always teaching at the edge of the unknown. It helped students to change too by playing into their various creative strengths, learning styles, and interests. It was hands-on and performance based and some of them hadn't taken the responsibility for learning in that way ever before. What I like about what we did with the kids is that we said, Let's try it, instead of, We couldn't do it that way, even when it appeared that we really *couldn't* do it that way!"

We agreed that the days and the moments that seemed like failure opened us to our own learning process. The failures were good because they showed we were breaking new ground and creating learning opportunities. If something wasn't working right, we were learning. If something was working, we asked how we could do it better. Between classes, during our free hours, and after school we exchanged stories of the day's problems and misdeeds. We would brainstorm solutions and create minilessons. We came to agree that "teaching failure" is an oxymoron, so important and integral is failure to learning.

Maybe every educational experiment *is* doomed to succeed: even when it uses technology!

Just One More Try

CINDY HATT

"Literacy is developed as children engage with texts on a personal level, promoting their critical understanding of the text as well as their understanding of themselves."

I penned those words in a term paper for one of my courses soon after I began doctoral studies at the University of Maine. My vision for my second-grade classroom was so clear on paper. There would be ample opportunity for reading—whole-class read-alouds, small discussion groups, and individual silent reading. There would also be opportunities for students' personal response to stories through discussion, writing, art, music, and drama. I could hear the hum of young readers at work and see heads bent over books in concentration whenever I imagined myself back in the classroom. They would come to literacy through involvement with books, understanding text and themselves. Or at least, I planned it that way.

I've just finished another year of working with second graders and even though I know there were those opportunities for reading and response that I wrote about so clearly at the university, one morning keeps coming back to haunt me. I can still see myself stomping around the classroom like a madwoman, ranting and raving while twenty seven- and eight-year-olds looked at me with blank stares.

When I traded the world of the university seminar room for the elementary classroom, I was in a different setting with new characters and an ever-changing plot. Adults sitting around a table and calmly discussing the week's readings had been replaced by twenty children surrounded by paintings, posters, books, and insect collections—all the tools of primary classrooms. And I was the only adult for (what seemed like) miles around. Now the carefully discussed theories and beliefs had to be put into action, and they would have immediate consequences. There was little time for the luxury of rewording and rethinking during the busy rush of the day. It is one of these days that I would most like to revise and edit and then neatly package back into my teaching life.

I had been reading *The Three Little Wolves and the Big Bad Pig* (1993) to my second-grade class that day. This story is a takeoff on the familiar story of the three pigs, except the roles are reversed. The children's discussion surrounding the book had concentrated on finding similarities and differences between this story and the original as well as talking about the wolves' problem and how it might be resolved. I had decided to stop reading just after the pig came to the third wolf's brick house. In the traditional tale this is the end of the wolf's success in destroying houses, but in this story the pig dynamites the house to smithereens. The story goes on and the pig and wolves eventually reconcile, appreciate each other's cultural differences, and become friends. However, I wanted the children to record their predictions before they heard what the pig did to the brick house.

"What do you think the pig will do next?" All the good things this would accomplish flitted through my mind. They would be drawing on evidence in the text to predict the pig's action. They would be making intertextual connections between the traditional tale and this modern one. They would be imagining themselves in the story as they guessed at some appropriate action. Perfect—an understanding of the text and of themselves!

Then, as they began to write, the first question came. "How do you spell *play*?" PLAY, I thought, how do you spell play? It's April and you don't know how to spell play! What have I been doing? I know, I know, spelling shouldn't be a primary concern in first-draft writing, especially in response journals, but come on, PLAY?

The next child I sat with had *blow* spelled as *bowl*. I zeroed in on it, hardly reading the other sentences. "Listen for the sounds," I admonished. It never got any better. I started putting words on the board with the directive to "check to see which words you need." I went from child to child, pointing out spelling mistakes.

I was panicked! I was sure they had a better command of spelling than this. This was no longer related to the plight of the three wolves. This had become a test of my teaching ability, and I was feeling like a failure. I was frantically reading children's work, looking for anybody who was measuring up to my expectations. I became the big, bad wolf in the traditional tale, huffing and puffing and blowing houses down.

After what felt like an eternity I took a deep breath and went back to reading the book to the class. The rest of the morning was uneventful. It wasn't any surprise that nobody had written more than two sentences in their journal. Why should they, with me on the hunt for spelling mistakes?

I don't like myself very much when I think about that day. I let my uncertainties about how best to teach spelling cloud my perspective that morning. Maybe my standards for spelling accuracy had been too low all year long. Maybe I had taken too many things for granted. Maybe the children didn't care—I had to take the blame for that. It isn't easy to write about the days when we have such a low opinion of ourselves. I wish I could end by saying that I lived "happily ever after" with a new approach to spelling, but I can't. I did learn that when spelling became my focus it impeded the children's interest in writing. I was also reminded of my own insecurities regarding how best to teach spelling. Revisiting it now forces me to think about what works and what doesn't.

I know what didn't work—my act as the big, bad wolf. But what should my role be in giving the children more responsibility for checking their own spelling? And what strategies and environment do I need to concentrate on in order to turn over that responsibility? To help me arrive at some answers I brought all my spelling resource books home for the summer holidays. They're piled in a box sitting in a spare room. My plan this summer is to create a new vision of literacy, one that balances the primacy of meaning with the efficiency of conventions. I wonder if it will be neatly organized on paper like the previously well thought out plans. Or will I force on myself the luxury of rethinking and reworking, being content with first-draft writing for awhile? Once again I will plan my students' encounter with text to bring them to literacy. And I'll try not to huff and puff—just one more try.

Reference

Trivizas, E., and H. Oxenbury. 1993. *The Three Little Wolves and the Big Bad Pig*. Toronto: Scholastic.

Got So Much Responsibility

RUTH SHAGOURY HUBBARD

It's the physical symptoms that are the hardest, in a way. A wavering shaky unevenness in my voice matches a spot in my stomach that is grabbing harder and harder. Vision clouds as my eyes fill with tears that threaten to overflow. My body betrays the intense emotions that I'm struggling to keep hidden. The worst of it is, I'm standing in front of a class of twenty-five students. Maybe that's the *second* worst of it: the horrifying, embarrassing, totally awful *worst* of it is, I'm not a beginning teacher struggling to learn to deal with a group of unruly adolescents. No, I'm a veteran teacher—a teacher of teachers—on the verge of completely losing it with a class of student teachers.

What am I doing standing here with emotion radiating from me, facing a room of inquisitors, and feeling as if I am on trial for my life with no chance of acquittal?

It didn't come on suddenly; it's been building, gaining momentum over the last few weeks: Grumblings and tensions about the rigors of the program as the students take on more and more teaching responsibilities. Worries about the job market. And most difficult for me to hear, complaints about the curriculum: a program that stresses a learner-centered philosophy yet continues to enforce certain requirements and assignments.

Though I started the fall term with high hopes and good spirits, it didn't take long to realize something was wrong—maybe even a lot of somethings. The interns weren't engaged with the materials or the format of the class. The feeling of camaraderie and "we're in this together" that holds a class together wasn't growing. I was troubled, but not terribly so; I optimistically thought the situation might prove to be a valuable teaching tool. I could model what *they* might do when they need to solve problems with their classes.

So I made time for class meetings. We brainstormed what was working and what needed to change. Or rather, we tried to. We seemed to end those sessions hopelessly mired in where to go next. The class was dividing into factions: either "make more class time to talk about these issues, since this is the crux of education" or "stop all this discussion and navel gazing and get on with the class." I agreed with both and neither. I felt that I knew the direction we needed to head, but couldn't seem to communicate it. Here was a group of bright, talented young people, committed to becoming teachers. When I was driving or trying to sleep, I would rerun classes, conversations, and missed opportunities in my mind. They deserve better, I told myself. Maybe I'm not the right person to work with this particular group. Instead of the usual average age of around thirty-five, this group was composed of mostly twenty-three- and twenty-four-year-olds, fresh out of college. I loved the intensity and vitality they brought to our classes, but I was feeling helpless to channel it in positive ways. I appreciated the diversity of opinions and philosophies they brought, from conservative Christian beliefs to leftist leanings, but I wasn't succeeding in making class a safe place to air these views. I talked to teaching friends, made plans and changed plans, and continued to fail.

Some teachers have a special connection with certain age groups and work best with them: it seemed that early adulthood was *not* that "special group" for me. What was wrong with me? Why couldn't I adapt to meet the special challenges and opportunities of these students? Then a new, dark thought began to form: wait a minute! Maybe it isn't me . . . it's *them.*

They're too young and full of themselves to teach, I told myself. One of my colleagues, who was struggling with them in similar ways, agreed. "You shouldn't be allowed into an M.A.T. program unless you've had two years of real-life experience after school," he told me.

"With some exceptions?" I offered.

"Of course, exceptions—if they've had at least two traumatic experiences. Divorce counts as one."

Protected by the veneer of my sarcasm, I decided I had found the answer. They had unrealistic expectations—of the graduate program, of their students, and of me. They didn't understand the realities of the teaching world, where there's too much work and too little time, where you always have to compromise. They didn't grasp the delicate balance in a student-centered philosophy between student choice and teacher responsibility. I have a responsibility to send out only really good new teachers, I reminded myself. I have to think of the generations of students they'll affect over the life of their teaching careers. Most of these students aren't ready to be the kind of teachers our schools need.

"And they're mean to each other," I told another friend, who teaches high school. "They don't listen and help each other. How are they going to listen to their students, to the parents, to their administrators, for heaven's sake? If they can't listen and be kind to each other, how can they possibly be effective teachers?"

She listened patiently, then asked, with lifted eyebrows, "And you've been to how many faculty meetings over your career, Ruth?"

She was right, of course. The way we act with our peers isn't necessarily the way we act with our students. A teaching faculty, just like a graduate class, brings together an assortment of personalities, political beliefs, cultures, and temperaments. We find our niche within that group—at some times more comfortably than at others. Blaming my students for their differences, for their age, and for the ways they coped with the stress of their responsibilities wasn't the answer either. But I couldn't just give up and wait for the year to end. It was only January! I had to do something.

Time to give "the negotiated curriculum" another try, but this time in a more structured discussion format, I decided. Before our Monday afternoon class, I listed the state requirements for certification that were a part of this course (The Structure of Knowledge). Since they were in a program that led to Oregon state certification, these assignments must remain—but we could devise different approaches and ways to meet these goals. I also listed other requirements of the course that were open to revision based on their suggestions.

It started off well, but like our other well-intentioned class meetings, it soon began to fray at the edges. We made some decisions about easy aspects, such as making their weekly journals optional. But when we turned to other more important decisions, the discussion completely unraveled. I became the lightning bolt representing every unhappiness with the Program (note the capital *P*). Complaints ranged from the lack of a student lounge to the unreasonable teaching and courseload expectations to the fifty-dollar placement fee. My resolve turned to defensiveness and finally to anger.

That's when I lost it.

"Okay, that's it," my unsteady voice proclaimed. "We've made a few minor revisions in this course. I've given you the opportunity for larger changes, and instead of doing that, you've only whined and complained. Well, I won't waste any more class time on this. If you have suggestions for changes—as individuals or groups—great! Come and see me in my office and we'll talk about it. But I won't listen to complaints about things like placement fees—would you think it's fair for your students to complain to you about gym fees? What do you think, I used that money to buy new curtains for my house? I've had it. And I mean it! *(Pause)* I'll see you Wednesday."

With that, I fled the room, straight to my office to collapse into self-incriminations for my ridiculous lecture, my embarrassing retreat, and what felt like the hopelessness of my current situation.

That night I drank coffee and listened to music late into the night, until the words of Stevie Forbert's "Responsibility" allowed me to empathize more with my students. Though he was singing about the pressures on a top-notch rivet crew, he might as well be singing about educators, who "don't get time to pace ourselves; we don't stand around and dream." We feel the overwhelming weight of our students' lives—and their possible lives. My interns were dealing with making the transition between *being* students and having responsibility for their own students. And I was struggling with the burden of worrying about my responsibility to the interns themselves, and to their students. These responsibilities are real. They don't wipe away the equally real problems we were experiencing, but at least they make them more understandable.

When I returned to class the next Wednesday, I carted along the Stevie Forbert tape and copies of the lyrics to "Got So Much Responsibility." I told my students that when I listened to the song, I knew I had to bring it in to share it with them, and to dedicate it to all of us. We listened—and for a change, *didn't* talk about it. Tentatively, we moved on.

I wish I could say that day represented a turning point. Though some of the tensions and difficulties went underground, they continued to erupt over the course of the year. It will live in my memory as the most difficult teaching of my life. I still find myself re-creating narratives of the year's events, assigning responsibility for the problems slightly differently each time—to personalities, curriculum, systems, politics. Even now, several years later, I'm not sure what I would do differently. Still, I learned that my failures with that group of students didn't signal the end of my teaching days—I've lived to experience successes since then (and yes, often with twenty-three- and twenty-four-year-olds). I found I could survive even the humiliating experience of publicly losing it with my students. Though I may not have learned how to deal with a similar failure in the future, at least I know can live through it!

Naked in the Hallway—
And It Wasn't a Dream

ANDRA MAKLER

t's funny how memory works. It's both easy and hard to recall my first year of teaching. 1978 is seventeen years ago, so I can be excused if some of the images are dim. However, some images do not blur with time; they retain an exquisite clarity. My "new teacher" nightmares still have that clarity: standing in front of the class with all my buttons undone; the principal dropping in unannounced when my class is totally out of control; a student's saying or doing something awful to another student. Some things that actually happened were too bizarre to dream up. Like the time in U.S. history class when enthusiastic seniors acted out the 1968 Democratic convention and brought a pig to class to run for President. Or the afternoon that Jason and Sam stood outside my classroom door naked except for grass skirts. To his credit, the vice principal, who "just happened" to be walking the hallways, did not burst into the room demanding to know what was going on; he waited until the end of the period to summon me to the office.

I was hired during the ninth week of the first semester to replace a popular social studies teacher who decided he was "burned out" and wanted to try his hand at writing. Sociology was a second-semester elective. That gave me nine weeks to familiarize myself with the class sets of readings neatly stacked in the closet of my new classroom. It didn't particularly bother me that there was no textbook for sociology. Although this was my first teaching job, I had an M.A.T. degree, I was thirty-six years old and had three kids at home, and I wasn't going to bore my students with worksheets. I was going to engage them in meaningful learning. They would "do" sociology, conduct surveys, consider issues of social class; they would be involved.

I spent hours viewing every film available through the school district with a title that hinted at relevance to a social studies class. I came across a series of videotapes about the research of an African American sociologist from Harvard. The videotapes chronicled the norms, customs, and way of life of South American villagers in a remote setting. I thought the videotapes would show students that people we liked to call "primitive" had good reasons for behaving as they did in their environment. In short, I was counting on the videotapes to reinforce the academic message that simple village life was as complicated as our own, that all societies relied on the same social institutions (family, some form of government, religious and spiritual ideas and practices, education, and ways of earning a living).

I prepared my students well to derive meaning from those videotapes. They knew how to define culture (the shared way of life of a people); they knew that norms were enforced by sanctions, positive and negative. Oh, yes, they learned the lingo. They wrote essays explaining that although our child-rearing and educational practices might differ from the villagers', the villagers' practices made sense given their cultural values and the environment in which they lived.

I wasn't teaching that all cultures were "equal" or equally good; I was trying to teach the idea that cultures make sense to those who live in them. I wanted my students to understand that people from other social groups or nations might judge us according to their norms and values, as we judged them according to ours. No longer would my students make the mistake of labeling strange customs "dumb."

In keeping with the educational theory I had so recently been studying, I gave no test. Rather, I asked students to develop small-group presentations that would "show" the sociological concepts and theories we had been studying. As I recall, I divided the class into groups of four or five; each group had a card with instructions. Sam and Jason were part of the group that was told, "You are sociologists who have just returned from studying the life of this small isolated village deep in the jungles of South America. Drawing on your work in this class, develop a five- to ten-minute presentation of your research." What the rest of the class did is a blur, but I clearly remember Sam and Jason's presentation.

Sam and Jason were inseparable. They enrolled in sociology because they needed a social studies credit to graduate. They were seniors who belonged to the "subculture" of stock car racers, and they loved to remind me that their main reason for coming to school was to finish the airplane they were working on in science.

Discipline in that science class was tight, expectations were clear, and success or failure was clearly visible: either the plane flew or it didn't. Sam and Jason weren't sure about me or my teaching methods; but sociology had a reputation for being a "better" elective than international relations (which required participation in an extracurricular activity called Model United Nations). Along with others, Sam and Jason had grudgingly conceded that an assignment that asked them to categorize the norms, values, and sanctions important to their family had given them a different perspective on their relations with their parents. Thus, they were willing to suspend disbelief long enough to at least try whatever bizarre assignment I made during normal class hours. They conferred with their group and agreed to be ready "to present" the following day.

Neither Sam nor Jason appeared for attendance taking at the beginning of class, but others assured me they were getting ready for the group presentation, which was organized as a public TV–type television show. Sam and Jason were to be interviewed by the other members of the group. The group members came to the front of the room and placed chairs in a semicircle. The "host" announced the start of the TV show and introduced the group as university researchers who were going to talk with village members recently arrived from the jungle. (I recall feeling a slight tinge of panic when I heard this introduction.)

The door flew open and in bounded Sam and Jason: bare feet, grass skirts, bare chests, and bones wound into their hair. I was dumbfounded. I felt my face flame red. They jumped around the room, grunting, scratching their arm pits, behaving like human beings imitating chimpanzees. The "university researchers" herded their subjects up to the front of the room and proceeded to translate their grunts into English for the benefit of their classmates. Laughter erupted, spontaneous, merry, unbridled. Then the noise died. The room became unnervingly still. Chairs creaked as students turned to look at me. I sat frozen in my chair in the back of the room.

Avoiding eye contact, I sat thinking, This can't be happening to me. How could they do this to me? This was worse than any teaching story I'd heard during student teaching. The class was clearly out of control. I had lost them forever. What was I going to do? I could not hide under the one-arm desk I was seated at, but I could leave the room. I could also stand up and say something, but what?

Should I stop the group from finishing? Rant about the idiocy of this presentation? Try a classroom meeting and ask for student input? Explain why I was upset? Tell Sam and Jason how disappointed I was that they had resorted to stereotyping, then ask their classmates to label all the things about their presentation that were wrong? Let the presentation continue and hope some brave student would risk peer disapproval to criticize the stereotyping?

The Sam-and-Jason show was grade-C Hollywood, far worse than Saturday morning cartoons. If I interceded, would I risk losing students' trust forever? Would they feel their classmates had been set up, ridiculed? Wasn't this to be expected when a teacher encouraged student creativity and didn't lecture and do worksheets? If I didn't do something, would they leave class believing sociology was all a crock? What would the rumor mill make of this incident by the end of the day?

I write the above as if I calmly sat in my seat and reviewed my options. I was not calm. I was close to a state of panic. I was breathing hard. My face burned. I am sure I was beet red. I wasn't sure I could control the tears welling in my eyes. I felt betrayed. I also was angry at the kids for taking advantage of my trust. I was scared that I had lost all control of this class, that I would be revealed as . . . not a "real" teacher.

Some place inside my head a small voice began to make sense: If you believe all the theory you profess, then you should see this as a teachable moment! It's up to you to make it teachable. What's going on here? Ask the class! Go ahead: Ask the class! What's going on here? See whether what they've been writing in essays and saying in discussions is what they believe, or whether they've just been "giving the teacher what she wants." Trust them. Ask them to explain what is going on.

It felt like time had stopped. I cleared my throat. Again, every head swung to look at me. Jason and Sam stood still. My voice shook, but I managed to ask, "What's going on here?" No one spoke.

I asked again, "What do you see happening? What are Jason and Sam showing us about our socialization, our culture?" Someone said something about stereotypes. I asked where we learned those stereotypes. More silence. My face continued to burn. Then Jason and Sam spoke up. They admitted they had based their performance on cartoon images, on Hollywood movies rather than the videotapes seen in class. They had wanted to have some fun; there were no minorities in the class, what harm was done? We began to talk about the power of stereotypes, of images, of the media, about how hard it was to get rid of the myths you learned as a kid. The class was "saved."

But I remained shaken. Rather than a creative lesson that engaged students' "sociological imaginations" and induced attitudes of sensitivity to other cultures, that lesson almost became the catalyst for reinforcing the very opposite of what I hoped to achieve! I learned more about the power of early socialization than the students did. I learned that there were some risks I didn't want to take again. And I learned that the vice principal was willing to suspend judgment until he heard my mea culpa. He also extracted a promise to implement some accountability checks on student creativity the next time I made an open-ended assignment.

Learning from Unexamined "Good Ideas"

HEIDI MILLS

The first group of Eisenhower Grant teachers grew out of our local Teachers Applying Whole Language (TAWL) support group. We met once a month to explore theoretical and practical issues related to literacy growth and instruction. We had been working together in the context of TAWL for several years and wanted a vehicle for working intensely and collaboratively on interdisciplinary curriculum through teacher research. It was marvelous! Our time together is frozen in most of our minds as being the most stimulating and professionally satisfying in our recent history. We all stretched. We all exceeded our own and one another's expectations. It was in fact what we could legitimately call "curricular heaven" (Hannsen 1992).

A couple of years later, we wanted to repeat this experience and decided to pursue Eisenhower funds for support once again. This time we knew we wanted to include teachers from the original group who were interested but also knew that it was our responsibility as teacher educators to extend our thought collective beyond the sheltered walls of TAWL. At the same time, we were being encouraged to work with local schools that had been identified as Professional Development Schools. In an attempt to meet internal and external demands on our time, we decided that a model highlighting the original teachers as "teacher-leaders" would make perfect sense. And it did, until we began making decisions that made the model seem exclusive rather than inclusive.

We began the year with an inspiring institute that featured the original group of teacher-researchers. We wanted the new teachers to experience firsthand the power and potential of the projects they were about to embark on. And they did, until about halfway through the day when they began feeling overwhelmed and insecure about their abilities to teach and research in the ways the first group did.

In an attempt to make the new group feel secure and comfortable and in an effort to continue to stretch the original group, we decided to form homogenous inquiry groups! We thought it made sense to provide the new group with the same kinds of experiences the first group had undergone. We planned demonstrations and engagements focusing on

Introduction to whole language.

The authoring cycle as a model for inquiry.

Math and children's literature, etc.

While the new group was experiencing what I now think we perceived as prerequisites for inquiry, the original group explored such issues as

The tentative nature of knowledge.

Content versus inquiry perspectives on learning.

Sign systems and knowledge domains.

Multiple ways of knowing, etc.

Basically, we were addressing very practical issues with the new group and exploring sophisticated theoretical perspectives with the original group.

It happened so easily. It seemed so right while being so wrong. And the sad thing was, once we made the mistake to offer separate meeting times and course assignments the first semester, the groups never functioned as a unified whole. We did not build a strong cohesive community across groups. Therefore, although we planned joint meetings during the spring semester, both groups functioned as separate entities who were simply sharing the same time and space. The new group of teachers never felt comfortable sharing questions, concerns, or even their expertise with the original group, because they were not connected to them and oftentimes intimidated by them. The original group of teachers seemed to seek out colleagues from their own group as well and unintentionally signaled the new group that they needed to be with the "advanced group" to learn.

While everyone did grow and enjoy their time together, Dave, Amy, and I continually struggled to connect the groups. We believed that all the teachers had a great deal to teach one another regardless of prior experiences. We believed that a strong sense of community was essential for genuine learning to be fostered. We believed that our actions reflect our beliefs and that reflection is essential to growth. Unfortunately, our decision to divide the groups and the significant time lapse between our actions and our reflection on the ways in which we were violating our own beliefs meant lost opportunities for genuine collaboration and growth for us all.

As whole language teachers, we naturally look at the world through rose-colored glasses. Our observations and interpretations are not naive or uninformed. Instead, we simply adopt an optimistic attitude toward teaching, learning, and our learners. We have found it to be most informative and inspiring to learn to "look for and value what is there." While many other prominent models focus on deficits, our model helps us see promise and possibilities. Such a positive stance serves us well in most circumstances. However, it is a bit misleading. Simply because we have intentionally adopted a holisitic model of learning doesn't mean that we will experience "curricular heaven" each and every day of our professional lives. It also does not ensure a critically reflective stance from which to critique and grow from our mistakes.

Taking a Second, Closer Look

There were lots of reasons to celebrate:

- We were promoting classroom inquiry within the Professional Development School network.

- We were providing graduate credit, classroom materials, and professional literature to dedicated teacher-researchers.

- We were bringing nationally known consultants to our area so that teachers who were unable to attend national conferences could work closely with some of the "big thinkers" in the field.

- We were inviting teachers to pose and investigate their own research questions within the context of their own classrooms.

- The teachers had a great deal of choice and ownership in selecting readings and course assignments.

- We were providing opportunities for them to explore strategies for developing an integrated, inquiry-based curriculum.

- We were supporting a "teachers teaching teachers" model by inviting the original group of teacher-researchers to share their expertise with the new group of participants.

While the list of positive features of the experience could go on and on, I am embarrassed to admit that although it is shorter, my list of concerns or reasons not to celebrate affected and restricted the learning potential of *all* of the items in the first list.

Reasons not to celebrate:

- We violated our model by *separating the two groups of teachers* for many of the first-semester meetings.

- Although we were promoting heterogenous grouping in elementary and middle school classrooms, we were homogenously grouping the teachers based on their prior experiences or knowledge base in whole language, inquiry-based instruction, and teacher research.

- Although we were advocating the value of multiple perspectives on issues in public school classrooms, we were acting as if there were a core list of prerequisite objectives that teachers needed to accomplish before becoming "teacher-leaders." We acted as if the new group needed to go through the same experiences the original group had to understand whole language/inquiry well enough to have thoughtful and productive conversations with the "teacher-leaders."

While I am astonished at this mistake, it is a telling example of why bad things happen to unexamined "good ideas."

Reference

Hannsen, Evelyn. 1992. Personal Communication at Research Roundtable. National Reading Conference. December, 1992. Charlestown, SC.

Practicing What I Preach

MARK W. F. CONDON

ccording to the Bible, pride goes before a fall. The most precipitous
fall in my teaching career came about eight years ago, on an evening
when my "very professorial" lesson plan for my twenty-plus graduate
students was designed to be thoughtful and responsive, scientific yet flexible.
It focused on one of my favorite ideas—kidwatching (Goodman 1978), the
careful observation of learners to support curricular decisions. This is a particularly relevant topic for this story, as my personal failure at watching *my*
"kids" that evening resulted in a week or two during which I sincerely wondered whether I would be permitted to continue my teaching career.

As the evening progressed, I was pleased to be leading a lively discussion
regarding how to observe children scientifically, especially those who are very
guarded or disinterested in sharing who they really are. In the middle of our
lesson, Shirlene (a pseudonym, obviously), who was sitting almost opposite
me in our circle of learners, mumbled something and began to rise, eyes
darting about the class. She was trembling as she looked heavenward and, in
a moan that ended as a shriek, said, "Oh, God! Someone help me!" Her short
dark curls were quivering and her eyes stared into space through oversized
glasses. She reached out and placed her palms on the table as if to retain her
balance as she rose.

I sensed this must be some kind of medical emergency, so, attempting
to display a measure of "withitness," I began to cross the room, though in
the first few steps I hadn't quite formulated anything to say. As I gestured an
offering of assistance, she continued, "I don't think I can take it any more!"
It occurred to me briefly that my lesson wasn't going as well as I had first
thought and that I had really badly confused some key idea in my presentation. However, that notion passed quickly as she went on, "Oh, Jesus! What
am I going to do?!"

Students on either side of her, in a class consisting mainly of experienced professional women, began to reach out gently to her. (I was somewhat

169

relieved that no one made any attempt to better explain the points I had been making about observing children.) They attempted to support her physically as she teetered in front of the group. A few more of us were now standing. "Please, please, hold hands with me!" she wailed, signaling us to link hands in a circle around the room. Her classmates obliged as I tried to decide what to do next. My instinct was to keep her from any danger and just let her inform us of her needs. Her needs, however, were not those that I was in any way prepared to address.

In the middle of leading a professional discussion about sensitivity to subtly expressed learner needs, I realized that though I knew the woman's name and school, I (whose expert status as a kidwatcher was quickly eroding) knew nothing more about her. All I knew was that she was clearly in some kind of crisis and that in my utter ignorance about her, I, the teacher, was without any strategy for supporting her. "Please kneel with me and pray," she urged the group that now was holding hands in a nearly complete circle.

I was in the middle. The words seemed to reverberate throughout the room . . . "kneel" . . . "pray." Now, I do not subscribe to any particular religion. For me, this is professionally acceptable; I work happily in a non-sectarian state-supported institution. I do have what I glibly refer to as my spiritual side, but organized religion and I went our separate ways many years ago. However, I have always remained in awe of people with deep faith or religious conviction. Not that I can relate to much of the focus of their fervor, but I have always envied the thrill and the comfort that so often accompany the faithful, regardless of the deity or prophet involved. Shirlene's last words knocked any sense I had about appropriate public school leadership tactics totally out of my head.

As the word *pray* slowly sank in, heads rotated away from her and fixed on me. Apparently, it was my decision whether, in this state-supported university, we should pray together at the request of a student in obvious distress. Everything began to move in slow motion, and with my professional life quickly passing before my eyes, I considered the request.

In flashback, I saw myself as a kindergarten child. I was at the Christmas program in my one-room kindergarten-only school, back in the early fifties. An entire room of Ward and June Cleavers, sitting forward on creaky wooden folding chairs, their faces reflecting our cellophane-wrapped flashlight "candles," were watching *me*. Their eyebrows arched in support of my attempt to sing solo *and* a cappella, all eight verses of "The First Noel." The candles reflected on the shiny red bows cinched up under each child's chin. Heads held erect, all of my scrubbed and coiffed classmates were facing their families. However, they also seemed to be looking at me, awaiting the cue I would offer for the next chorus. The cue never came. At age 5.7, three verses into what inexplicably remains a favorite carol, I experienced my first total stage fright, forgot everything my mother and I had practiced for two months, and began to cry.

I then heard myself say, "Those of you who would like to, could certainly join Shirlene in prayer." As I had done in kindergarten more than forty years before, I turned and walked out of the spotlight. In December 1951, my teacher had thrown her arms around me and consoled me in my misery. This night I was alone. I turned back to discover that Shirlene had indeed found supportive people with whom to pray, and I then exited the room, relieved that both Shirlene and I were, at least for the moment, still alive.

I wonder if all those years before, had my breakdown been anticipated by a capable kidwatching teacher and I had somehow been taught how to appropriately communicate my need for help, I might have been able to finish that song. Alas, just like my teacher before me at that pivotal moment, I was not in a position to understand or support my student.

The praying didn't last long. I muttered that it was break time for what used to be my class. The "congregation" began to filter out of the room into the hall where I stood. The group was whispering as if they were exiting church, but the eyes of my disciples all said, What is going on here?! Though as confused as they, I nodded with a slow blink, offering each of my students an I've-got-everything-under-control look that rarely fools anyone. I reentered the room; Shirlene was there with a few kind souls who, though in the dark about her situation, murmured vague blessings of generalized comfort. She saw me and with a look invited me to join her. As I did, her remaining attendants left. I invited her across the hall into my office, where I offered her some water and the telephone to call anyone she would like. I asked whether she might wait there until after class so we could talk. She seemed to find the small space agreeable and as I pulled the door nearly shut, I could see her blinking repeatedly as her thoughts changed from here to wherever her troubles were and back again.

When my students returned from their break, I told the class that I was sorry if anyone was upset by the events of the evening. Lacking energy and direction, the class ended early. Later, in the quiet office, Shirlene shared her impending unwanted divorce and her troubles at work and with her teenage son.

By the end of our discussion, the importance of the class topic that night had been forever emblazoned in my mind. Here was a woman who was on the edge of breaking emotionally. Though I could discuss in the abstract how learner-centered curriculum is appropriate and how careful kidwatching was at the center of all good teaching, I had never imagined this to have anything directly to do with me in my role as a teacher educator. As happens periodically in classrooms everywhere, that day the students taught the teacher a thing or two.

I took scant solace that Shirlene had found something in my class inviting enough to "share" her troubles with us all. But it had been an occasion for me to be the learner and to accept that universal truths about good teaching include me in their universe. All learners, from preschoolers to postgraduates, must be met where they are, understood, and offered appropriate bridges to connect their knowledge, background, values, and feelings with the curriculum.

I spent the next few days sending explanatory, even apologetic memos. It felt as if I wrote to everyone in the state, from members of my department to the governor, hoping not for success but merely to save my job and perhaps my face. The good-natured "Reverend" used before my name in the following weeks let me know that I was going to be fine and would likely remain employed as a professor. It seems that no one was bothered much but me.

Shirlene returned the following week but never mentioned that evening. She was quiet, guarded as usual in class, showing little about who she really was, taking notes of some kind, and smiling approval for comments made by her less reserved peers. After that class meeting, she never returned. At semester's end, I gave her an X for the class, administratively documenting that she was "still working" on some part of the curriculum.

I hope that Shirlene remembers me in some positive light, the way I remember my kindergarten teacher. Though I remember little else about 1951, I remember my teacher as supportive and accepting and wonderful at a time when I needed it. She was at a loss to bring me to finish that song, just as I failed to anticipate Shirlene's crisis, to support her, even to finish the class. It seems that neither of us has finished that class.

Perhaps, as with long-lost friends, the teachers we remember fondly are viewed in more global ways than for particularly well structured lessons or specific instructional events. We continue to embrace them despite their inadequacies and their personal idiosyncrasies, despite times when we may have been let down, as I was by my kindergarten teacher and as Shirlene was by me.

In the rush of daily activity at my university, I still struggle professionally to "see" my students clearly and to accept them as being fully human, unique individuals whose lives include many more important aspects for their consideration than anything in my curriculum. Although the "science" of my teaching may fail me as a professional educator, the art of consistently caring for my students as fellow human beings and learners cannot. Without such humanity, what good is science anyway?

Reference

Goodman, Yetta M. 1978. "Kidwatching: An Alternative to Testing." In *The National Elementary School Principal*, 57, 2: 41–45.

Pay Attention, Roy

KATHY G. SHORT

C ome on, Roy, pay attention. Please follow along on the page." Trying to get Roy engaged in what we were doing in reading group (or at any other time of the day) had become a daily chore. I tried pleading, coaxing, and threatening, but nothing seemed to work. Roy came to the reading group and sat there with his book open along with the other first-grade students, but that was the end of his cooperation. He refused to use his finger to follow along as others read from the story. His mind always appeared to be elsewhere. He turned the page when the others did, but he rarely glanced at the print and never knew where we were on the page when it was his turn to read.

I encountered Roy early in my teaching career. Even though much of my teaching was fairly traditional at that point, I was a creative teacher who brought in many supplementary activities and books. I cared deeply about my students and they responded positively to the learning engagements in the classroom, even those (such as the reading groups) that were boring. While I had students who were disruptive or struggled as learners, I had never had a student who simply chose not to engage. Roy made no pretense of being involved. He didn't fool around. He didn't disobey or defy me. He completed what he needed to. He just chose not to invest anything of himself in experiences unless they were something that he found personally interesting or meaningful.

I tried everything I could think of to reach Roy. I called in his parents for a conference and they helped me understand part of the problem. Roy was their only child and they wanted life to be easy for him. Despite living on a farm, Roy was given no chores or responsibilities. Everything was done for him. Learning to read was probably the first time Roy had ever been asked to struggle at something. He didn't expect to have to put out effort and so he simply didn't. His parents and I agreed that they would give him some chores and responsibilities at home.

I brought in books about farms and animals that I thought might interest Roy and made them available to him during our sustained silent reading time. He did spend time looking through these books. Still when reading-group time came, he was unresponsive. I had him sit next to me and shared a book with him, running my finger under the print to help him see where we were reading or taking his finger and guiding it as we read. I threatened him with having to stay in from recess (his favorite time of the day). I tried joking around with him. I tried ignoring him. Nothing worked. He came to group each day, opened his book, and disengaged his mind.

We ended the year much as we began. I could see no noticeable change in Roy's behavior. He was reading, although not as well as most of the other students, but he still refused to engage during our reading group. During the rest of the day, his attentiveness varied. There were times he engaged in activities with the other students, especially during our theme units, but often he made only a halfhearted attempt—enough to complete the task but with no real thought or effort.

As he left the classroom on the last day of school, I felt a sense of defeat. A whole year and I couldn't tell that there had been any change in his behavior or perspectives toward school and learning. Where had I gone wrong in reaching him? I was extremely surprised when several weeks into school the following year his second-grade teacher told me that if she heard my name from him one more time she was going to scream. According to Roy, I could do no wrong. I looked at her in surprise and talked about my frustrations in working with him during first grade.

I've often thought about Roy and wondered what happened. I still feel defeat about his lack of engagement and surprise that he thought highly of me. His actions in first grade had never conveyed those feelings toward me. I continue to puzzle over why he chose not to engage, although as I've learned more about reading and inquiry processes, I have a better sense of the complexity of issues affecting his responses. Roy did not accept the work ethic that says you need to work hard at whatever tasks are placed in front of you no matter what they are. For Roy, those tasks had to be meaningful. He didn't want to read stories from the basal so that someday he could be a good reader and read books that interested him. He wanted engagements and books that were meaningful to him now. If there wasn't something he could immediately gain as a learner, then it wasn't worth the effort.

Because Roy wasn't willing to play the "school game," I wonder what became of him. In many ways I hope that he never gave in and played that game, because his insistence that school make sense in his life is one that could serve him well as he makes his way through society. If more of us insisted that our work and lives make sense, the world would be a better place. On the other hand, I worry because I know that those who don't play the school game often end up dropping out because of the lack of flexibility within the system. My fear is that he either finally gave in and played the game of school or was tossed out of the game and left school.

As I puzzle over Roy's responses, I realize that there are many ways that children "drop out" of school. Having a highly structured, direct teaching environment doesn't ensure that children will be thoughtfully involved in learning activities. We can force children to be present in our classrooms, but we can't force them to engage their minds meaningfully. No matter how "on task" their behavior appears to be, they determine whether they engage their minds or simply go through the motions of what we ask as teachers. Students can pass quizzes and complete all worksheets and assignments and still choose not to engage thoughtfully in those tasks. We have no control over that as teachers. We can create environments that encourage students to think deeply and critically, but the student is the one who chooses whether or not to actually think.

It is a common tendency for us as teachers to dwell on those students who don't connect no matter how hard we try to reach them. On one hand, we overlook the many students who are connecting and are engaging thoughtfully and critically. On the other hand, I have learned the most about myself as a person, learner, and teacher by trying to understand those students who don't connect. While my feelings of defeat are often an overreaction, those students whom I don't understand are the ones that push me the most as a teacher. As an inquirer, I know that when I focus on the "yet to be understood," I will develop new understanding and new questions that will allow me to continue in an endless cycle of inquiry and growth.

Irony and Teaching: Three Students, Three Stories

TIM GILLESPIE

Mr. Gillespie!"

I'm downtown one Saturday, and a voice skids across the sidewalk. I turn around. A tall young man, on the upper edge of his twenties, strides toward me with his hand out. Behind his mature face I see a younger face: a student who used to be in a class of mine a decade earlier. By some miracle a name comes to me.

"Dwayne?"

"Hey, Mr. Gillespie." He pumps my hand enthusiastically. "Geez, I can't believe you remembered me."

Me neither. "Well, Dwayne, you'd be hard to forget!"

Dwayne laughs. And as I watch his face, I remember more. He had longer hair back then. More details come: he was antsy, curious, eager, always ready to talk. He had a hunger for ideas, I remember. I appreciated his jittery zest and responsiveness; he'd give things a go. An enthusiast for new ideas. No wonder I remember him. Dwayne.

"I remember your English class, Mr. Gillespie."

"Yeah, what'd you take, junior English from me?"

"No, I had you senior year."

"Ah."

"You know what I remember?"

"What?" I'd like to know.

"Irony."

"*Irony?*"

"Yeah, that was so cool." Now Dwayne gets serious. "I remember you talking about irony being a commentary on the gap between the way things ought to be and the way things are, you know, like between the ideal and the real." He gestures with his hands, the way you'd show the size of a fish you'd almost caught. "Irony, you said, is the twist of things, like a reversal that

176

shows our grand expectations to be absurd or pitiful. It's, like, a clear look at the state of modern craziness."

I am astounded at this street-corner recitation. I hear a vaguely familiar echo of words I might have said a decade ago.

"So I see life with an ironic viewpoint, Mr. G. Because of your class."

"Ah." I think of a line from a Grace Paley story about the kind of remarks that can bore their way, like a plumber's snake, from your ear down to your heart. This is the way Dwayne's remarks work on me. Meanwhile, we talk about his job, his plan to marry his girlfriend, his news of old buddies. Then we say good-bye, and he walks away. I stand there stupefied.

Of all the things we must have talked about the year Dwayne was in my English class, of all the things we read and wrote and discussed, why on earth, I wonder, would a definition of irony be the one thing he remembers? Why would *that* stick with him? Is irony the most memorable intellectual tool I've passed on to my students? I'm surprised how much this thought distresses me.

Perhaps this is because I worry, as teacher and parent, about our contemporary inclination for irony. Our culture is thick with irony; it's our habitual postmodern response to the complexities of modern life, our comfortable armor, first cousin to cynicism.

So is this what I'm teaching? Am I contributing to the great undertow of alienation and nihilism among young people? I want students to understand irony, but I do not think irony is a sufficient response to life. Irony offers a sort of clear-eyed realism, but it's not the critical analysis nor the attitude that it takes to work for a better world. I want Dwayne to remember English class for other lessons and stories, too, for the tales of heroism and hope that can inspire us, the dramas of other people in other places and times that can cultivate our sense of empathy and moral imagination, and the images of truth and beauty that can hold us steadfast in the face of modern craziness. Literature offers many attitudes and viewpoints toward life, so I'm sorry that irony is all Dwayne remembers.

As I walk downtown, I weigh the effects of my encounter with Dwayne. On the upside, Dwayne has remembered my class with great affection, and something he learned there has stuck with him as an important insight for over a decade. Yet I feel oddly uncomfortable about what he has kept and cherished. Talk about ironic, I think.

Fast-forward a dozen years, to this past fall. I'm at a different high school in a different school district, teaching another senior English class. I'm having my students read *Oedipus Rex* after some introductory study of the Greek theater and Aristotle. As we begin to read together in class, I'm moved as I usually am by the powerful dramatic irony of Sophocles' play. The students start with a wariness for this ancient work, but over a couple of days most of them seem to warm up to the play. Many volunteer to read parts, and we have rich discussions. Then, however, it is the Wednesday before Thanksgiving, and five days before I next see the students. When we return, we pick up where we left off reading. But something has been lost; the pace lags; we stop to discuss and the class acts sluggish and resistant.

"What's wrong today?" I ask, trying to kid my students into loving what I love. "We seem dead in the face of this great piece of classical literature. Are you experiencing post-Thanksgiving stress syndrome or something? Are you still digesting that big meal? Or, hey, maybe it's the turkey. Isn't there some chemical in turkey—serotonin or something—that makes you sleepy? Maybe that's our problem today."

Jacob, the most remote and uninvolved student in the class, ever in danger of flunking, looks up. For one of the rare times during the year, he actually appears about to speak. I am exultant. So far, I have pretty much left Jacob alone about his withdrawal from classroom life, sensing that he might respond better to patience and breathing room than to confrontation. And now he seems about to speak. Finally. Other students perk up, curious about this rare occurrence. "Mr. Gillespie," he says, holding his copy of *Oedipus* in the air, "*this* is the turkey."

The class laughs, applauds, cheers, and I laugh. Greg turns to Kelly: "Now *that* was ironic."

Now, I realize this scene should stop here where it's funny, but it doesn't. Stories in life don't always end where we'd like them to. In fact, Jacob dropped out of school a couple of months later.

"Why?" I ask him.

"I don't know," he replies. "There's just nothing here for me."

"Could I have helped, or done more?"

"No, this class is probably as good as they come, but . . ." He looks at me and shrugs.

I am relentless; this is the way I deal with the disappointment. I wonder why I wasn't this engaged with Jacob before he made this decision. "Was there *anything* we did in English that was meaningful to you?"

He shrugs and looks away, and then offers his own bit of irony. "I remember," he says, "that time I made a joke in class that made everyone laugh."

Fast-forward once more to this past spring, just before graduation. On the day I hear that I was voted favorite teacher by the senior class, I open a letter from one of the most gifted student writers I have ever had. Chloe, who rarely spoke in class for reasons I never clearly understood, had initiated a series of letters to me during the year, writing whenever she wanted to comment on some issue in the literature we were reading or on some remark I had made in class or on a paper. A bit stumped by her silence, and wanting to encourage whatever communication I could, I would respond at length to each note.

We corresponded this way, by letter, about once a month all year. I was knocked out by the eloquence and insight of Chloe's letters and thoroughly enjoyed the correspondence, though I always hoped she would share more of her opinions aloud during class discussions.

Her final letter of the year was the one from which I will learn the most. Chloe wrote, in part, "I think you really don't understand me at all. . . . Very often in class discussions, you interrupt people before they have made their points. Unconsciously, perhaps, you use the beginnings of people's ideas to launch into your own anecdotes so that by the time you've finished, the class has forgotten that someone was trying to express some insight, and that person may have lost his or her fragile grip on a delicately budding idea. I see a great deal of eagerness and exuberance behind these interruptions, and these qualities I admire. Unfortunately, any passion that goes unchecked can destroy its object—in this case, the atmosphere of learning and discovery."

"Congratulations on your teaching award," a colleague stops by to say, just as I am finishing Chloe's letter.

"Uh, thanks," I reply. The air is thick with irony. Chloe's remarks bore their way toward my heart, like that plumber's snake. Like the truth.

Dwayne, Jacob, Chloe. Teaching is not primarily pedagogy; it is these young people and all the others, names and faces attached to beating hearts and eager brains. Have I served these students? I want to find successes in my experiences with them. After all, I tell myself, Dwayne did remember with great enthusiasm what he learned in my class. And Jacob did move an entire class to laughter and acclaim with his wit. And Chloe did write with insight and clarity, and I believe that my responses supported her honesty. But these interactions are painful in memory for me, too. I wonder about my mistakes; I wonder about the awful results: Dwayne is an ironist, Chloe went unheard, Jacob just went.

So, what *do* stories of classroom mistakes teach? What have I learned from these three students? I rethink my teaching, and wish I would have played each of these scenes differently, but I'm not sure exactly how. Clear lessons don't come easily; there are incongruities that crash against any generalizations I might make. Maybe Dwayne needed a broader focus for his enthusiasm, Jacob more of my enthusiasm, and Chloe less of my enthusiasm and more of my listening. But even that little formulation sounds too pat and glib.

Thus, I don't have a homily, conclusion, or wise lesson for my teaching life that I can easily extract from each experience. The stories have their ironies, but irony isn't sufficient to help me be a better teacher. At best these experiences offer a bit of clear-eyed realism.

Many other students have left me with many other stories, most not so perplexing, but these three I will carry with me for the way they complicate my thinking and learning as a teacher. Each reminds me that teaching victories and teaching mistakes twine together, weaving their lessons in that gap between the way things ought to be and the way things are.

References

Arnott, Peter, ed. 1960. *Sophocles' Oedipus the King and Antigone.* Arlington Heights, IL: Harlan Davidson.

Paley, Grace. 1974. "Wants." In *Enormous Changes at the Last Minute.* New York: Farrar, Straus & Giroux.

About the Authors

JAMES A. BEANE is a professor in the National College of Education at National-Louis University. His work is in the areas of curriculum design and democratic education.

BILL BIGELOW teaches high school history in Portland, Oregon. He coedited *Rethinking Our Classrooms: Teaching for Equity and Justice* (Rethinking Schools 1994) and is an editorial associate with the journal *Rethinking Schools*.

GLENDA L. BISSEX teaches a yearlong case study course in Northeastern University's Institute on Writing and Teaching and works with teacher-researchers in other contexts as well. As a learning specialist at Goddard College in Vermont, she tries to practice what she teaches.

MARY BURKE-HENGEN, after a decade at the middle school level, now teaches at Jefferson High School in Portland, Oregon, where she was given an opportunity to integrate global studies and world literature into one course. She is the author of several articles and chapters and is coeditor with Tim Gillespie of *Building Community: Social Studies in the Middle School Years* (Heinemann 1996).

KIMBERLY CAMPBELL is currently on leave of absence from her teaching position so that she can work with a small school district to develop—and it is hoped build—a new high school. She still finds time to read.

PENELLE CHASE coteaches a primary multiage group of children with Jane Doan. Together they wrote *Full Circle: A New Look at Multiage Education* (Heinemann 1994). Penny lives on a farm in Freedom, Maine, with her husband Addison and daughters Phoebe and Meg.

ELIZABETH CHISERI-STRATER teaches at the University of North Carolina at Greensboro where she directs the English Education program.

This is the first time she's been able to combine working with students from small rural towns and minority students from the urban area of Greensboro. Her book *Academic Literacies* (Heinemann 1991) is an ethnographic study of college students' reading and writing across the disciplines.

LEILA CHRISTENBURY is a former high school English teacher now at Virginia Commonwealth University in Richmond. The editor of *English Journal*, her most recent book is *Making the Journey: Being and Becoming a Teacher of English Language Arts* (Heinemann 1994).

LINDA CHRISTENSEN teaches at Jefferson High School in Portland, Oregon. She is an editorial associate for *Rethinking Schools*. Linda also serves on the steering committee for the National Coalition of Education Activists and is a member of the National Council of Teachers of English reading commission.

MARK W. F. CONDON began his life in education as an English and remedial reading teacher and for the past nineteen years has been at the University of Louisville in the Department of Early and Middle Childhood Education. He is currently teaching courses in literacy teaching and learning and inquiry for teachers K–12. His current research interests include collaborative authorship and the relationship between the school disciplines and inquiry.

PAT CORDEIRO is an associate professor at Rhode Island College, after teaching elementary school, grades 1–6 , for eighteen years. She is the author of *Whole Learning: Whole Language and Content in Upper Elementary Grades* (Richard C. Owen 1992) and editor of *Endless Possibilities: Generating Curriculum in Social Studies and Literacy* (Heinemann 1995). She learns from her teaching at her home on Cape Cod.

AMBER DAHLIN is an assistant professor of English at Metropolitan State College of Denver, Colorado. She is also codirector of the Colorado Writing Project.

JANE DOAN has been teaching and learning with children for more than thirty years. In spite of these years of experience and her coauthorship of *Full Circle: A New Look at Multiage Education* (Heinemann 1994), she believes her studies are nowhere near complete.

CURT DUDLEY-MARLING is professor of Education at York University in Toronto, Canada. His work focuses on the literacy development of struggling students and the politics of literacy. During the 1991–92 academic year Curt took a leave from university duties to teach third grade.

BOBBI FISHER is a first-grade classroom teacher at Josiah Haynes School in Sudbury, Massachusetts. She is the author of *Joyful Learning: A Whole Language Kindergarten* (Heinemann 1991) and *Thinking and Learning Together: Curriculum and Community in a Primary Classroom* (Heinemann 1995).

DANLING FU, a former English professor in China, is now an assistant professor in the Department of Instruction and Curriculum, College of Education, University of Florida. She also works in both elementary and secondary classrooms as a researcher and serves as a bilingual-literacy facilitator in San Francisco Unified School District.

JUDITH FUEYO, assistant professor of language and literacy at Pennsylvania State University, teaches graduate and undergraduate classes in language arts, writing research, emergent literacy, portfolio evaluation, and teacher as researcher. Her research interests focus on ways of knowing and alternative assessment.

MARNI GILLARD left her middle school classroom after almost twenty years to pursue a career in storytelling and writing. She coedited *Give a Listen: Stories of Stoytelling in School* (NCTE 1994) for the National Council of Teachers of English and recently published *Storyteller, Storyteacher* (Stenhouse 1996).

TIM GILLESPIE teaches English at Lake Oswego High School in Oregon. He has been director of the Oregon Writing Project at Lewis and Clark College and is past president of the Oregon Council of Teachers of English.

MICHAEL GINSBERG is an assistant professor of reading at Jefferson Community College in Louisville, Kentucky. A former newspaper reporter and sixth-grade teacher, he earned his Ph.D. in language education at Indiana University, Bloomington.

JEROME C. HARSTE, better known as Jerry or just plain Harste, teaches reading and language arts methods courses at Indiana University in Bloomington. Currently he is involved in several educational reform projects.

CINDY HATT has completed her doctoral studies at the University of Maine and is currently working with second and third graders at Rothesay Park Elementary School in New Brunswick, Canada. The well-thought-out spelling program has yet to be committed to paper but there has been no second sighting of "the big bad wolf" in her classroom.

CARYL HURTIG, a writer, consultant, and educator, is currently the coordinator of the Graduate Core Program at Lewis and Clark College (Portland, Oregon). As a charter staff member of the Oregon Governors' School for Citizen Leadership, she has worked with the institute since 1990.

JANE A. KEARNS, the preschool-to-grade-12 writing coordinator for the Manchester, New Hampshire, public schools, trains teachers in the process of teaching writing. She is a writing consultant and taught nine summers at the New Hampshire Writing Program. A secondary English teacher for twenty years, she remembers every one of her classroom disasters.

JANICE V. KRISTO is a professor of literacy at the University of Maine where she teaches courses in reading, language arts, and children's literature.

MARY MERCER KROGNESS, teacher/writer, has recently authored *Just Teach Me, Mrs. K: Talking, Reading, and Writing with Resistant Adolescent Learners* (Heinemann 1995). Mary, who wrote and produced *Tyger, Tyger Burning Bright*, an award-winning writing series for PBS, has authored numerous articles and chapters, including publications in *Language Arts* and *English Journal*.

BARRY LANE is a writer who spent the last five years teaching teachers and students about writing. His books and tapes include *Discovering the Writer Within, After THE END* (Heinemann 1992), *Writing as the Road to Self-Discovery* (Writer's Digest 1993), and *Lane's Recycled Fairy Tales* (revised fairy-tale songs for children).

On good days, ANDRA MAKLER is delighted to teach in the teacher education program at Lewis and Clark College (Portland, Oregon). On not-so-good days, she thinks about retiring to a book vault and overdosing on fiction and poetry. On most days, however, she is pursuing her interest in language and inquiry and musing about teachers' and students' concepts of justice, a current research interest.

CYNTHIA MCCALLISTER has taught grades K–5 in New York City and rural Maine. The experience of the incorrect correction, together with a wealth of other elementary-classroom teaching experiences, has shaped her insights about teaching and learning. Cynthia is an assistant professor of education at Muhlenberg College where she teaches courses in literacy education and educational foundations.

DOLORES MILLER has been a high school science teacher for thirty-two years. She is currently chair of the science department at Alden (New York) Senior High School.

HEIDI MILLS is an associate professor of elementary education at the University of South Carolina. She has devoted her career to collaborative inquiry, working closely with whole language teachers interested in expanding our vision of literacy and instruction. She spent four years working in Timothy O'Keefe's first- and second-grade classrooms. *Living and Learning Mathematics* (Heinemann 1991) and *Looking Closely: Exploring the Role of Phonics in One Whole Language Classroom* (NCTE 1993) emerged from their classroom research.

DONALD M. MURRAY no longer teaches in the classroom but he writes a weekly column for *The Boston Globe,* poetry, and fiction and shares what he learns in his books on writing and teaching writing.

SUSAN OHANIAN, a longtime teacher, now writes about education. Her most recent books are *Who's in Charge: A Teacher Speaks Her Mind* (Heinemann 1994), *Math at a Glance: A Month-by-Month Celebration of the Numbers Around Us* (Heinemann 1995), and *Ask Ms. Class* (Stenhouse 1996). She lives in Charlotte, Vermont.

JILL OSTROW teaches a class of first through third graders in Oregon. She has written a book called *A Room with a Different View* (Stenhouse 1995).

GLENNELLEN PACE coordinates an elementary preservice master of arts in teaching program, and teaches language and literacy and children's literature courses at Lewis and Clark College in Portland, Oregon. Her current research interests include middle-grade learner- and inquiry-centered democratic classrooms and schools.

MEG PETERSEN is an assistant professor at Plymouth State College (New Hampshire) where she works with writers and teachers at all levels.

JOANN PORTALUPI and PEGGY MURRAY are graduates from the Ph.D. program in reading and writing instruction at the University of New Hampshire. They have been collaborators in both the education department and the Learning Through Teaching program at UNH.

TOM ROMANO teaches in the Department of Teacher Education at Miami University in Oxford, Ohio. He is the author of *Writing with Passion: Life Stories, Multiple Genres* (Heinemann 1995) and *Clearing the Way: Working with Teenage Writers* (Heinemann 1987).

ROSEMARY A. SALESI is a professor of education at the University of Maine with responsibilities in teaching children's literature and writing process. She is also site coordinator for the University of Maine Center for Reading Recovery. Dr. Salesi is coeditor of Book Beat, a book review column in the *New England Reading Association Journal,* and a member of the Orbis Pictus Committee of the National Council of Teachers of English.

PATRICK SHANNON is grateful that he is still paid to teach—now at Penn State University and at the State College Friends School two mornings a week. His most recent book, *texts, lies & videotapes* (Heinemann 1995) uses stories about his life as a student, parent, and teacher to refocus the debate about schooling from test scores and high skill to the question of how we wish to live together.

KATHY G. SHORT has focused her work on children's literature, curriculum as inquiry, and collaborative learning environments for teachers and children. She is an associate professor at the University of Arizona where she teaches graduate courses in children's literature and curriculum in the Department of Language, Reading, and Culture. She is coauthor of *Creating Classrooms for Authors and Inquirers* (Heinemann 1995), *Creating Curriculum* (Heinemann 1991), and *Talking About Books: Creating Literate Classrooms* (Heinemann 1990). She coedits *The New Advocate,* a journal concerned with children's literature and issues related to its use in schools.

KIM R. STAFFORD is the director of the Northwest Writing Institute at Lewis and Clark College and the author of *Having Everything Right: Essays of*

Place (Confluence Press 1986). He holds a Ph.D. in medieval literature and teaches writing wherever he can.

After years of teaching and a period of time when she was codirector and co-owner of a small private school, JANE TOWNSEND is currently a professor of English education at the University of Florida at Gainesville where she teaches courses in writing, language arts, and language acquisition. Also, she has been investigating ways to support real discussion in school and to encourage wondering, exploratory thinking among students and teachers.

HERMAN G. WELLER taught science, mathematics, and computer programming courses for thirteen years in grades 8–12. He now teaches undergraduate and graduate science education courses in the College of Education at the University of Maine in Orono.

JEFFREY D. WILHELM has spent the past thirteen years as a teacher, first in high school English and then in middle school language arts as part of an integrated teaching team. His interest is in creating literacy opportunities for reluctant students through the use of technology and the arts. He currently teaches in the literacy area at the University of Maine in Orono.

Index of Themes

College Level

New-Teacher Blues

Collaboration and Community

Science and Technology

Ask Ms. Class

SUSAN OHANIAN

If you're like millions of teachers everywhere, surrounded by university pedants, curriculum zealots, school board buffoons, and driven parents, and you wonder how you'll ever get through it, you'll enjoy knowing Ms. Class.

Ms. Class is the source of sound advice for teachers. She deals directly and honestly with the questions teachers ask, as you will see in this collection of her outspoken letters of advice that will make you ponder, gasp, and cheer. And laugh!

In hundreds of letters Ms. Class covers all the important things about schooling and curriculum that concern you and those pervasive, trivial, but niggling details that *really* bug you.

Ask Ms. Class is the ultimate advice book, for Ms. Class knows that teachers don't want field trip frenzy, merit pay, vouchers, time-on-task slips, vowel extra-strength formulas, or scope and sequence free agency clauses. Teachers want to be heard.

1-57110-25-3   Paperback

*For information on all Stenhouse publications,
please write or call for a catalogue.*

Stenhouse Publishers
P. O. Box 360
York, Maine 03909
(207) 363-9198